To Lou & Kelly,

See, it is real!!!!

Love,
Terry

1-800-COURTESY

Connecting With a Winning Telephone Image

TERRY WILDEMANN

Aegis Publishing
796 Aquidneck Avenue
Newport, Rhode Island 02842
401-849-4200
www.aegisbooks.com

Library of Congress Catalog Card Number: 98-33554

Aegis Publishing Group, Ltd.
796 Aquidneck Avenue
Newport, RI 02842

International Standard Book Number: 1-890154-07-5

Printed in the United States of America.

10 9 8 7 6 5 4 3 2 1

Library of Congress Cataloging-in-Publication Data

Wildemann, Terry, 1955–
    1-800-courtesy : connecting with a winning telephone image / by Terry Wildemann.
        p. cm.
    Includes bibliographical references (p.).
    ISBN 1-890154-07-5 (pbk.)
    1. Telephone in business. 2. Telephone selling. 3. Telephone etiquette. I. Title
HF5541.T4W55   1998
381'.1--dc21   98-39172
                                         CIP

Contents

CHAPTER FOUR 91

Phone Management: Who's Winning. . .You or the Phone?

CHAPTER FIVE 105

Teleconferencing

CHAPTER SIX 123

Working From Home

CHAPTER SEVEN 141

Contagious Enthusiasm: Catch It and Pass It On!

RESOURCES 144

Acknowledgments

I received a phone call from my friend Renee Fullerton, director of the Rhode Island Homebased Business Association, asking that I pick up some donated books from Bob Mastin, owner of Aegis Publishing Group. The books would be distributed to the association's membership at the next meeting where I was booked as the guest speaker. Little did I know that this errand was about to change my life.

Imagine my surprise when a simple errand turned into a three-hour meeting after which I was holding a book contract. My head was spinning! For two weeks, I was filled with fear, elation, and awe. Then I got down to business.

This book would not be in your hands if it were not for the help and support of some special people. Thank you...

Renee Fullerton for your incredible networking skills. Your talent of putting the right people together is a rare gift. Mike and Ingrid Turner, of Kal-Tech Consulting, for your creativity with the titles. Eileen Santos, Karen Marlow-McDaid, and Alison Hamilton for listening and inspiring me at every turn. Jim Tinkham for your input and attention to detail. John Pantalone for being a terrific writing coach; you taught me so much. Francis "Nim" Marsh for being such a super editor. Dee Lanoue for fine-tuning the manuscript. Bob Mastin for your incredible patience, support, encouragement, and most importantly for your faith in me to produce a book that would meet your expectations.

Mom, Dad, and my siblings Lil and Ron for just being there for me during some trying and soul-searching times. To all of the special souls and guides in my life. I am forever grateful for your insight, vision, and wisdom. You know who you are. The most important thanks goes to four special people who gave me unconditional love and support and gave up so much to allow me to complete this project—to my husband Walt, my daughters Briana and Celina, and my son Jonathan. I dedicate this book to you because without your patience, encouragement, and inspiration, this book would never be. I love you.

Introduction

Do you know how to use a telephone? Sure, most of us have been making and receiving phone calls since we were children. Many of us feel as though we go through our lives with a phone plastered to our ear. But have you ever stopped to wonder whether you're using this valuable tool to its greatest potential?

Are you making the best impression you can on the telephone? Do you deliver your message effectively on the telephone? Are you losing valuable business or damaging your reputation with customers because of your telephone habits?

Most people enjoy getting mail. Occasionally one of those too-good-to-be-true mail offers catches your eye and you wonder... Well, wonder got the best of my friend Mary when such an offer from a prestigious magazine arrived in the mail. For the price of one subscription, Mary and four of her friends would receive six issues for a year. Since Mary picks up the magazine occasionally, she decided to check out the offer by calling the number listed in the advertisement. What she heard, when the phone was answered, wasn't quite what you would expect from such a celebrated magazine. Loud rock music assaulted her ears, and the voice of the person who answered was barely audible.

As Mary explained why she was calling, it became clear that the receptionist didn't have a clue about the offer. The receptionist stated that she would have to inquire within the office for more information and proceeded to drop the phone, adding insult to injury to poor Mary's ears. Mary was not amused. Any prestige the magazine may have had went right out the window with that call.

Companies spend millions of dollars yearly on marketing campaigns designed to persuade the public to buy their products. Yet when someone calls with an inquiry or to purchase their product, they don't back up their marketing effort by training their personnel in proper phone usage. How many customers did the magazine lose by not having trained and knowledgeable receptionists answering the phone? Yes, the offer was a good one, but there was little credibility established in the first precious seconds of that call.

The purpose of this book is to help you, and every person in any organization, learn telephone skills that will enable you to use this valuable tool, and its network, to its fullest potential. Read the classified ads and you will find that many customer service positions require good interpersonal communication capabilities and phone skills. Where do people get their training? Most schools don't teach telephone skills, so when the young graduate is hired, who trains him or her in the proper business usage of the telephone? No one, and it shows. Occasionally, someone answers the phone well, but midway into the call skills dissolve and lack of professionalism shows through.

People can't see you when using the phone so you must rely on your words and your tone of voice to get your professionalism across to the caller. Knowing what words and phrases to use when dealing with clients gives you a competitive edge. People are tired of being treated poorly, and the company that evokes a professional telephone image—one that makes customers feel they are special—will reap loyalty and profits.

Come learn how to connect with a winning telephone image that tells the world how wonderful you and your organization truly are. In this book, you will learn:

- How to demonstrate your respect for the customer on the telephone.

- How to turn unhappy or angry customers into satisfied customers.

- How to modulate your voice to make a winning impression on the telephone.

- How to recognize, within the first few seconds of a call, your customer's style of communication.

- How to tailor your message to the customer's style so that the customer will hear, understand, and believe it.

- How to work with emerging telephone technology, use faxes effectively, present a polished image on videoconferences, and use cell phones safely and courteously.

You have one chance to make a great first impression—whether in person, in writing, or over the telephone. This book will help you make sure that first impression—and every impression after it—is a successful one.

ABOUT THE AUTHOR

A respected trainer, speaker, image consultant, and businesswoman, Terry Wildemann, C.C.S.E., works with organizations and individuals to improve their professional and interpersonal skills. Her many clients include the U.S. Air Force, British Gas, the U.S. Navy, The Robbins Company, and The Preservation Society of Newport County. She has taught at Brown University, the Roger Williams University Center for Professional Development, and the Swinburne School, and has facilitated workshops throughout the Eastern U.S. and England. A resident of Middletown, Rhode Island, Terry has owned and operated Image Plus...® Associates since 1987.

Terry Wildemann
Specialist in Human Potential
Image Plus...® Associates
Tel: (401) 847-9291 or 1 (877) IMGPLUS 1 (877) 464-7587)
Fax: (401) 846-0678
E-mail: Success@Image-Plus.com
Web site: www.Image-Plus.com

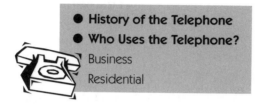

- History of the Telephone
- Who Uses the Telephone?
  Business
  Residential

CHAPTER ONE

The Telephone and the Network That Ties It Together

HISTORY OF THE TELEPHONE

It's difficult imagining our society without television—a society in which you could not watch the news or your favorite ball game, soap opera, or movie. Likewise, it's hard to envision a business world without the telephone and the network that ties it all together. Thanks to the telephone, we have technological advantages today that were unimaginable just over a century ago.

We so often take the telephone for granted. It rests unobtrusively on desks and walls throughout the world, but what a worker it is! It allows us to order a pizza or a sub, buy an outfit, furniture, window siding, or new kitchen cabinets—simply by dialing a few numbers. With the telephone we can speak to relatives three thousand miles away or chat with friends next door. In an emergency, we can dial for help in an instant with 9-1-1. Telephones thoroughly influence the way our society functions and how we interact; like threads in a tapestry, they are tightly woven into the fabric of our lives.

It all began on March 10, 1876, when Alexander Graham Bell said to his assistant over the world's first telephone, "Mr. Watson! Come here! I want you!" Bell's six little words started a worldwide revolution in communications and commerce.

Decades later the telephone's sibling, the facsimile machine (fax), arrived. It was the brainchild of H. Nyquist, who in 1918 began investigating methods of adapting telephone circuits for picture transmission. AT&T introduced the first fax, called "telephotography," in 1924 by sending 5x7 photographs from Chicago and Cleveland to Manhattan. Each took seven minutes to transmit.

Inventors and scientists then asked the question: If still images can be sent over a wire, why not moving images? Sounds reasonable, don't you think? That question led to the birth of another telephone offspring, the television, which was introduced in 1927. Live TV images of Secretary of Commerce Herbert Hoover were sent over telephone lines from Washington, D.C., to an auditorium in Manhattan in the first public demonstration in the U.S. of long-distance television transmission.

So many new technologies have been developed from the invention of the telephone. We are still in the adolescent stage of understanding how far these technologies will take us. For now, however, it is important to learn how to use the telephone properly.

WHO USES THE TELEPHONE?

A better question might be, who *doesn't* use the telephone? Search for a telephone and your journey will not take you far. You can find them on street corners or highways, in cars or restaurants, in markets or malls, in schools, or in backpacks, briefcases, or pockets. People wearing everything from business suits to swimsuits walk the streets (and beaches) talking on cellular phones. In our high-demand world, the telephone is no longer a luxury. It's a necessity.

Business

It's halftime and your alma mater's basketball team is leading by twenty points. As you sing your school fight song, you prance into the kitchen to make a mouth-watering ham-on-rye sandwich with lettuce, tomato, and a dab of mustard. Your taste buds scream as you imagine that luscious first bite. You open the refrigerator door to take out the ingredients, but catastrophe strikes. There's only one slice of bread! You could make half a sandwich by slicing the one piece in half, but somehow it's not the same.

You can't build a great sandwich without two slices of bread, and you can't build a great business without a telephone. Think about how businesses use technology to communicate with customers. You have the standard letter, fax, and e-mail, which take time and effort to produce. The telephone is quick and easy and has the missing link that the other communication methods lack. That missing link is the human voice, the person on the other end of the telephone who can answer your question in a flash, the person who can hear your emotions and your needs in a way that the written form cannot convey. When you consider that 50 percent of all business is done over the telephone, it's easy to understand why telephones are the tools of choice for business communication.

Residential

The average American family juggles a mind-boggling array of activities every day. Between parenting, careers, and relentless children's activities, families are in perpetual motion trying to coordinate numerous activities at one time. Without an effective means of communication, the family schedule would fall into immediate disarray. The telephone allows husbands and wives the freedom to call each other throughout the day to check that schedules haven't changed. Since plans often do change, new plans can be formulated with the aid of the phone, ensuring, for instance, that a child will still get his ride home from school.

Having friends at different stages of parenting allows us to see how their telephone use changes as their kids get older. At the baby stage, the phone is often off the hook so that the ring doesn't wake up the child. At the toddler stage, parents are scheduling for playgroups and day care. When the kids reach school age, parents use the telephone to schedule rides to and from activities. During the teen years, parents might put a lock on the phone, add another line, or accept the fact that they may not see their teenager again without an added appendage. By the time children reach college, you just pray that they call once in awhile to say "hello" instead of asking for money.

In the workplace, adults must use the telephone in a professional manner because they are not only representing themselves, but also their employers. Unfortunately, most adults don't use this wonderful tool to its fullest potential because they have not been taught to do so. This book will give you the information you need to connect with a winning professional telephone image—an image that lets the world know that you and your company are Confident, Competent, Credible, and Congruent. It's called a "4C Image."

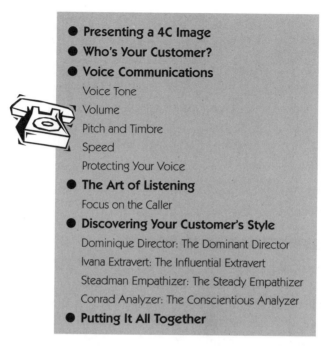

CHAPTER TWO

Using the Telephone to Win Friends and Influence People

We do 50 percent of our business over the telephone, so why don't we use the phone to its fullest potential? Why don't more companies present themselves positively when using this amazing tool? We take the telephone for granted and forget that this wondrous piece of equipment *by itself* is ineffective. Place it in the hands of people who use it poorly and business suffers. Put it in the hands of people who use it well, and they create positive connections that tell customers and colleagues alike that their organization has

> **Telephone image** can be compared with "road image" . . . having a car that represents how you want to present yourself.
> — **Merryl Carlsson**

the 4C Image of Confidence, Competence, Credibility, and Congruence (centered, clear, together).

PRESENTING A 4C IMAGE

Does it take work to present a 4C Image? Absolutely, and a lot of it! Everyone in the organization, from the boardroom to the mailroom, must take responsibility for the company's image. It's a never-ending process that, once achieved, must be nurtured and maintained. Let's take a quick look at what happens when Competence, Confidence, and Credibility are not working Congruently whether on or off the phones.

Salesperson A presents a confident and credible image, but isn't necessarily competent. He may present a great sales pitch and make the sale, but if he doesn't consistently process the necessary paperwork, orders become lost or never placed. Due to Salesperson A's poor follow-through, the company loses credibility and consumer confidence which directly affect the bottom line.

Coworker B is competent, but isn't necessarily confident. Have you ever shaken hands with someone who gives you a "fish" handshake? Yuck! Your first impression isn't positive, and it leads you to believe that she has no confidence in herself. In the course of working together, however, you realize she is a confident individual, but that she has never learned how to shake hands properly.

Caller C was referred to you by a colleague. He asks to

make an appointment in a quiet, shaky voice presenting a less than confident, competent, and credible impression. Upon meeting, you're surprised to discover that he is entirely credible and confident in person, but lacks confidence when working with the telephone.

The next scenario illustrates the 4C Image. You call a vendor to place a product order and the representative answers the phone in a confident, credible, and courteous manner. The agent takes your order quickly and efficiently. You hang up feeling positive about the interaction and wait to see if the order arrives as promised. It does, and without mistakes. The day after you receive your shipment, a company representative calls to make sure that everything was received as you had ordered and to ensure that the initial agent was courteous. You are so impressed with the company's service that you pass its name along to several colleagues who use the same products.

Presenting a 4C Image is hard work and takes lots of practice and mistakes to get it "together." However, it's a goal worth striving for, and anyone can do it with the proper training and a positive attitude.

WHO'S YOUR CUSTOMER?

There's more to projecting a winning telephone image than just learning "skills." Using new telephone skills without a thorough understanding of your customer resembles making chocolate milk without the chocolate. Something's missing. You must first identify your customer so that you can best apply the techniques that will deliver a winning telephone image.

When taking customer service training, participants are often taught that there are two types of customers: the external customer (your paying customer) and the internal customer (your coworkers). Many employers believe that to achieve success they must focus solely on pleasing the external customer. Under these circumstances, success is hard to come by and often at the expense of employees. That brings us to the internal customer: your coworker.

We don't usually think of our coworkers as customers but, in fact, they are easily as important as the paying customer. Since we spend most of our waking hours in the workplace, doesn't it make sense that we nurture relationships with the people with whom we spend so much time? Hal F. Rosenbluth, CEO of Rosenbluth Travel and author of *The Customer Comes Second*, puts it in simple language, "Companies must put their people first."

How can employees treat each other well in today's workplace environment if they are not treated with trust, honor, and respect by management? Parents who raise a child with patience and understanding prepare their child to be an adult who will trust, honor, and respect others in the workplace. Parents who raise a child with anger and distrust may lead that child into a life of misery and negativity. The workplace is no different. Management sets the tone for the organization. The workplace must nurture its people. We no longer have a choice. The world is filled with negative behavior, and we are all paying the price. It's time for all of us to take responsibility for change, and how we treat people over the telephone can make a difference, person by person and bit by bit.

Hal Rosenbluth states: "If more corporations paid as much attention to their people as they do to politics, public image, and increased profits, everything else would fall into place. Profits are a natural extension of happiness in the workplace. It doesn't work the other way around. We are consistently able to trace higher cost to cases of unhappiness in specific departments and offices. We (Rosenbluth Travel) take it very seriously."

A third customer may be the most important of all. This customer rarely thinks of himself as such and, as a result, lacks the respect due him. This special person is you. Confucius has said that by respecting yourself, others will respect you. If you don't respect and nurture yourself the way you would another customer, how can you expect anyone else to? You are at the core of customer service, whether it is great or poor, and people can feel it the moment you pick up the telephone or enter your office. When you respect yourself, you naturally respect your coworkers. When coworkers respect each other, then the paying customer enjoys a natural extension of that respect. It shows in job performances and, ultimately, in how workers treat the internal and external customer. Until you understand that customer service begins at "home," you will not be a successful salesperson whether face-to-face or on the telephone.

The following example illustrates how trust, honor, and respect in the workplace are keys to healthy and powerful communications that present winning images both over the telephone and in person.

Johnny Selfabsorbed has worked hard to be successful in his eight years as sales manager at Widget Express Company. Everyone at Widget knows Johnny. His reputation always precedes him.

Every morning at nine o'clock, Johnny enters the glass doors of the stately red brick office building that houses the Widget Express Company. While walking through the hallways, Johnny ignores his coworkers as he thinks, "I can't be bothered with these people since I don't need them to do my job." When he enters his department, everyone suddenly becomes quiet and avoids eye contact with him. Johnny is known throughout the company as a master of intimidation. Whenever you approach the doors of his department, you sense a heaviness in the air.

Walking toward his office, Johnny sees his administrative assistant, Patient Lucy, speaking on the telephone. Working for Johnny Selfabsorbed for the last two years has been an interesting experience for Patient Lucy. In a cold monotone, without regard for her telephone conversation, he demands his mail and messages. Johnny impatiently paces back and forth as Patient Lucy asks her caller, the human resources manager, if she can return the call. After hanging up the receiver, she hands Johnny the stack of mail that was just delivered by the mail attendant and several sheets of blue paper with clearly written messages. Johnny briskly takes them from her without any acknowledgment. He notices that Patient Lucy has the same sad expression that she wears every morning. He knows that a good office assistant is hard to find and that she delivers excellent work. As long as Patient Lucy does her job well, what she feels is of no concern to him.

Stepping into his office, Johnny notices that the cleaning staff did a good job, especially since he left the place a mess the evening before. Sinking into in his buttery-soft leather chair, Johnny begins to read his messages but is interrupted by the ringing telephone, followed by the intercom. Johnny presses the intercom button and answers with a perturbed, "Yeah?" Patient Lucy informs her boss that fellow executive, Dorothy Smile-A-Lot, is on line one asking to speak with him. Without saying anything else to Patient Lucy, Johnny clicks off the intercom. He sits back in his chair, knowing why Dorothy was calling.

Dorothy Smile-A-Lot, the manager of the marketing department, was recently honored with the "Manager of the Year" award. She has a company-wide reputation for being a fair, open-minded, and positive person. Dorothy runs her department with sensitivity and humor, maintaining high standards for both herself and her staff. People always leave the marketing department's office with a smile. She and Johnny don't see eye-to-eye on most things, though Johnny does admire her.

As Johnny picks up the telephone and says, "Johnny

here," he senses through the phone line that Ms. Smile-A-Lot is not smiling.

She asks, "May I speak with you a moment?"

Johnny responds with, "Yeah, what's your problem?"

After an ice-cold pause that feels like an eternity, Ms. Smile-a-Lot speaks in a strong, clear voice and says, "Johnny, we're late on the Rainbow Trout proposal because we haven't received your figures. When can we expect them?"

Johnny coldly remarks, "My secretary will give them to you this afternoon. That's the best I can do."

"Please remember, Johnny," says Dorothy, "that you promised us those figures last week. We cannot submit the proposal without them. Don't let us down. The Rainbow Trout account is one of our largest and best accounts. We don't want to lose them as a customer, so we must keep them happy."

Johnny sits back in his chair and begins to think about what to do to quickly get accurate figures for this proposal. First, he must contact Mark Moneyhead in the accounting department to research the figures. Then Sara Eaglebeagle in the legal department needs to review the documents before he turns the figures over to Dorothy Smile-A-Lot. Johnny says to himself, "They can drop whatever they are doing to help me. After all, my job is more important than theirs, and I need this information now."

Johnny gets on the intercom and says to Patient Lucy, "Call Mark Moneyhead and Sara Eaglebeagle and tell them to be in my office in fifteen minutes for a meeting."

Patient Lucy asks, "What if they are busy and can't make it in fifteen minutes?"

"I don't care what else they are doing. It's not important. Just make the calls," screams Johnny.

Patient Lucy rolls her eyes in exasperation and says under her breath, "Who does this guy think he is? He's not even their manager!" She picks up the telephone receiver to deliver the commands to Mark Moneyhead and Sara Eaglebeagle. As she is dialing, she thinks, "If it weren't for the great benefits and the pay, I would be long gone from this place."

Mark Moneyhead and Sara Eaglebeagle meet in the hall on the way to Mr. Selfabsorbed's office. Walking shoulder to shoulder, Sara whispers to Mark, "I despise it when Selfabsorbed calls. He treats you as if you don't exist. Then when he needs something, he expects you to drop everything for him. I have no respect for this guy."

Mark whispers back, "Everyone in this office feels the same way you do. I never like doing anything for Johnny Selfabsorbed. In fact, when he calls with one of his commands, I do what he asks, but it takes me twice as long. You should see him turn on the charm and shmooze with the customers. I'm sure they see right through him since his personal sales are behind last year's sales. If his clients only knew how he treats his coworkers, they might think twice about doing business with Widget Express."

You may be wondering what this story has to do with telephone skills. Actually, a lot, because how you communicate in person may correlate with how you communicate over the telephone. In the above scenario, Johnny Selfabsorbed communicates negatively over the telephone with Dorothy Smile-A-Lot and in person with Patient Lucy. His attitude costs him dearly because Johnny doesn't treat his coworkers and staff with trust, honor, and respect. His attitude that he can't be bothered with his coworkers is off the mark. That kind of negative thinking infuses all of Johnny's communication. He doesn't understand that he can't do his job well if:

- His office isn't clean. Thank you, office cleaners.
- His daily mail isn't sorted and delivered by the mailroom personnel. Thank you, mail clerks.

■ His administrative assistant doesn't schedule meetings, type letters and proposals, and take telephone messages. Thank you, Patient Lucy.

■ Accounting doesn't provide him with the numbers for his proposal. Thank you, Mark Moneyhead.

■ The legal department doesn't review the proposal so that it can be delivered. Thank you, Sara Eaglebeagle.

Unfortunately for Johnny, the distrust, dishonor, and disrespect with which he treats his employees and coworkers boomerangs. Walk into his office and you are surrounded by an uncomfortable negative energy. A quick look at the people in his department shows you an irritable staff hunched over phones with their heads in their hands. There are no smiling faces greeting you, and they respond to you as if you are an inconvenience.

Johnny is his own worst customer. No one wants to be in his company. His people work for him for the wrong reasons. Money isn't always enough to keep good qualified people if the environment they work in is stressful and they are unhappy.

Walk down the hall to Dorothy Smile-A-Lot's office and, before you open the door, you sense the positive energy emanating from the room. You feel welcome because the people are happy and content. They work in an atmosphere of trust, honor, and respect, and it shows. Whatever you ask them for is delivered with a broad smile. In Dorothy Smile-A-Lot's office, people perform because the standards are high, they enjoy their jobs, and they know that they are valued. This is what we call "Wow" service. "Wow" service gives customer care new meaning. It is essential at every level and in every department of any business. With very little effort, the end user—the paying customer—becomes the recipient of "Wow" service when it becomes integrated into an organization's culture. "Wow" service creates loyalty, and loyalty generates business.

To deliver "Wow" service, the internal and external customer need to feel listened to and know that their needs will be taken care of with a positive attitude. The adage, "the attitude you send out is the one you get back," is right on the money when it comes to relationships.

Now that you understand the importance of customer service on all levels, we can begin to focus on how to communicate well using the telephone.

VOICE COMMUNICATIONS

Most of us don't pay much attention to our voice. The reality is that your voice is a powerful instrument that creates vivid images in the minds of listeners. If telephone use is critical to your job, you must take care of your voice so that you can project a 4C Image and come across as the talented professional that you are.

To illustrate the power of voice image, take a quick look back in history to the early 20th century. When the "talkies" were introduced, many actors and actresses lost their careers because their voices didn't match the image they created in silent films. Research shows that listeners create opinions about a speaker's intelligence, educational background, authority, and truthfulness based on voice quality. A strong, clear voice, such as Yul Brynner's, creates an image of strength and power. A strange, squeaky voice, such as that of Pee Wee Herman, creates an image of insecurity and weakness.

Research shows that the communication process consists of visual, vocal, and verbal signals. According to psychologist Albert Mehrabian in his work, *Silent Messages: Implicit Communication of Emotions and Attitudes*, visual signals (body language) communicate 50 percent of your message; vocal signals, such as pitch, speech rate, and volume, communicate 38 percent; and verbal signals, or your words, communicate 7 percent of your message. When using the telephone, unless you are on a videophone or at a teleconference where you see the people you are speaking with, you automatically lose 55 percent of your communication power. Your voice image, together with good listening skills, is the key to presenting yourself well. It instantly tells how someone is feeling physically and psychologically. Let's take a look at the different elements of voice image and how they affect the vocal message.

Voice Tone

Do you remember as a child hearing your parents call out your name and, based solely on their tone of voice, you knew what was in store for you? My father's tone when I'd been bad made me jump. I'd get that queasy knot in my stomach that told me, "I'm in trouble again." On the other hand, whenever my dad came home from a business trip, he would say my name in a loving tone that let me know he'd brought me a gift.

Your voice tone over the telephone is no different, and it can create powerful images and feelings. Let's see what telephone image the sales associates from XYZ Toolhouse give you.

You're having trouble with a project, and you need a special tool that you don't have. You grab the Yellow Pages and let your "fingers do the walking" to find just the right source. A great advertisement catches your eye, so you decide to contact that company first. You pick up the receiver, listen for the dial tone, dial the number, and your conversation sounds like this . . .

> **Receptionist:** *"Heeeellooo."*
> **You:** *"Is this the XYZ Toolhouse?"*
> **Receptionist:** *"Yeah, what can I do for ya?"*

You: *"I'd like to find out if you carry a wire widget?"*

Receptionist: *"I dunno. I gotta ask Mike. Hold on, will ya?"* You hear in the background: *"Hey, Mike, do we have a wire widget?"*

Mike: *"Yeah, there's a couple in a box here but I gotta go on break. I'll talk to ya when I come back."*

Receptionist: *"Heeeellooo. Yeah, we have a couple of wire widgets here in a box."*

You: *"How much do they cost?"*

Receptionist: *"Why didn't ya ask me that before? Hold on again!"* You quickly pull the telephone receiver away from your ear as you hear the receptionist's phone crash against something hard.

Receptionist: *"Hey, Mike (pounding on a door), the guy on the phone wants ta know how much these wire widgets cost."* You hear a muffled voice say something you can't understand.

Receptionist: *"Mike says that they're $35 each. OK?"*

You: *"Thanks for your trouble."*

Based on the receptionist's tone of voice and the words she used, ask the following questions:

- What picture does this scenario paint in your mind?
- What do the characters look like?
- How do you see them dressed?
- What does the place of business look like?
- Is it a positive or negative image?
- Would you spend your money in that establishment?

- Did they deliver good customer service?
- Did you feel as if they wanted to do business with you?
- Did you feel like an inconvenience?

You can probably answer these questions quickly based on a two-minute conversation, which is about how much time the above scenario would take. Isn't it amazing how tone of voice, words, and attitudes can create powerful mental pictures? I call this "voice attitude." When listening carefully on the telephone, you can quickly decipher the feelings of the other person.

Let's do an exercise that illustrates how voice tone can change the meaning of a message. You are going on vacation and need to find a kennel for your beloved award-winning 100-pound Rottweiler and three cats. Using the phrases below, in your mind's eye paint a clear picture of what a person is feeling when he or she answers the telephone with the phrase, "Thank you for calling Chow Down Hotel. This is Barfy, how may I help you?"

- a tired voice
- a sad voice
- a panicked voice
- an exhausted voice
- a dead voice
- an admiring voice
- a feeble voice
- a surprised voice
- an anxious voice
- a confident voice
- a gentle voice
- an energetic voice
- a sleepy voice
- an angry voice
- a hearty voice
- a faint voice
- a boring voice
- a calm voice
- an excited voice
- a threatening voice
- an affectionate voice

If Barfy answers with a confident voice, that would speak favorably for the kennel. If Barfy answers in a surprised tone, I'd wonder why, which would make me anxious. If Barfy answers in a feeble tone, I'd take one look at my Rottweiler and imagine Barfy in flight holding onto the dog leash during a walk. What pictures do you get when you read each of the descriptions?

Volume

Volume indicates the loudness or softness of your voice. A loud telephone voice may cause you to pull the receiver away from your ear. A soft telephone voice may cause you to strain to hear the message. Both extremes cause the listener to become distracted and focus on the voice instead of the message. What picture comes to mind and what feeling do you get when you think of:

- a loud voice
- a thunderous voice
- a deafening voice
- a soft voice
- a quiet voice
- a raised voice

Pitch and Timbre

Pitch is the degree of height or depth of a tone or sound. Timbre is the characteristic quality of a sound independent of pitch or loudness. Your voice pitch and timbre reflect how high or low you speak and the quality of your voice. Fran Drescher of the TV show, "The Nanny," is famous for her harsh, nasal voice. Mickey Mouse has a high-pitched, squeaky voice. Disney's Cinderella has a soft, youthful voice. What picture comes to mind and what feeling do you get when you think of:

- a high voice
- a grating voice
- a raspy voice
- a shrill voice
- a velvety voice
- a childish voice

- a womanly voice
- a squeaky voice
- a piercing voice
- a robust voice
- a manly voice
- a screeching voice
- a metallic voice
- a muffled voice
- a mature voice
- a youthful voice
- a deep voice
- a hoarse voice
- a boyish voice
- a musical voice
- a nasal voice
- a smoker's voice
- a girlish voice
- a guttural voice

Speed

Listeners are distracted when people speak rapidly and mumble. When this occurs, the speaker may be nervous, stressed, or anxious. It may indicate a lack of confidence. Speakers who do this often feel they need to get their words out quickly before the listener loses interest. Telemarketers often do this, which is most aggravating.

I recently received a call from a telemarketer that was infuriating and disrespectful. She called on behalf of a credit card company that was selling protection service in the event my cards were lost or stolen. I tried to say that I was not interested in the service, but I could not get a word in edgewise. She spoke so fast, with an I-don't-care attitude in her voice, that I could not understand most of what she was saying. I think she said, "Mrs. Wildemann, with this service there is a free thirty-day trial period and if, at the end of that time, you are not pleased with the service, you can cancel at any time. I will submit your application, and we look forward to serving you."

The opportunity to accept or decline was never offered. I was able to catch her just before the call disconnected by saying, "I am not interested in this service." She continued her spiel, and I interrupted her to say again that I was not interested. Then she hung up. That was the worst call I have ever received from a telemarketer, and I complained to the credit card company. There is more on this type of call in the next chapter.

On the other hand, speaking too slowly can be equally distracting. The slow-speaking person may convey an image of tiredness, lack of interest, boredom, or unfamiliarity with the text he or she is reading.

Speaking too slowly or too quickly will impact your telephone image. How can you help yourself present a positive and powerful telephone voice? Tape record yourself. Play the tape back and listen to it carefully over and over again. Dissect it, and ask yourself if your voice sounds:

- too loud
- too soft
- too energetic
- too slow
- too young
- too old
- too high-pitched
- too low-pitched

Ask yourself if you are:

- speaking confidently
- sounding insecure
- speaking too quickly
- finishing off your words

You may not like listening to yourself when you play back the tape, but remember that you are hearing what your listener hears. Articulate clearly. If you find that you are chopping off word endings such as movin', runnin', or smilin', Art Sobczak of Business By Phone, Inc. suggests practicing tongue twisters. Reciting tongue twisters helps you to form complete ending sounds and enunciate every word.

A trend I find annoying is raising one's voice at the end of every sentence as though a question is being asked. Read the following, raising your tone in a questioning manner at the end of each sentence: *And we have this product? It's used by a lot of people? They say it's the best they've seen?*

The impact of such messages is diminished, and this bad habit is tough to break. A colleague spoke of this same annoyance in a recent lecture. Ironically, I have heard her speak in the same questioning fashion on more than one occasion. Today we laugh when I bring it to her attention.

Note if your speech is peppered with "ums" and "ahs." This practice signals that you may be uncomfortable with the topic you are speaking on. Practice, practice, practice until you no longer use ums and ahs in your speaking. It can be distracting and presents an unpolished image.

Protecting Your Voice

You have only one voice, so take care of it. If you make your living speaking over the telephone as a call center representative, salesperson, customer service representative, or if you just use the phone a lot, listen to the following cues that signal you may be headed for voice problems:

- hoarseness
- tension/tightness in throat
- sore throat during/after speaking
- weak voice projection
- tired voice
- dry, scratchy throat
- frequent throat clearing
- losing your voice

The following are some voice health care dos and don'ts adapted from a piece written by Clark A. Rosen, M.D. and Thomas Murry, Ph.D. of the University of Pittsburgh Medical Center. It was originally written for singers, but many of the following suggestions are appropriate for frequent telephone users.

DON'T

✓ Smoke tobacco or marijuana.

✓ Use drugs.

✓ Drink alcohol or coffee.

✓ Become a cheerleader.

✓ Shout and scream at sporting events.

✓ Go to loud clubs or bars.

✓ Try to be heard in noisy places such as bars, sport arenas, large family gatherings, airplanes, and buses.

✓ Vocalize a sneeze. This does not mean you should stifle a sneeze. Go ahead and sneeze; just don't phonate (produce a vocal sound) while doing so.

✓ Phonate while yawning.

✓ Cough.

✓ Clear your throat continually.

✓ Speak if it hurts to swallow.

✓ Try to talk over a cold or laryngitis.

✓ Speak higher or lower than is comfortable.

✓ Whisper loudly or for very long.

✓ Raise the chest or shoulders when inhaling.

✓ Be a vocalist in an acid rock or heavy metal band.

✓ Talk on a lower or higher pitch than is comfortable for you. The *huumm* pitch (expressing mild surprise) is the pitch at which you should be speaking.

✓ Try to change your natural speaking voice ("vocal image," e.g., sexy, macho).

DO

- ✓ Speak at your own pitch (like Julia Child and opera divas).
- ✓ Support your speaking voice just as when singing.
- ✓ Get plenty of rest.
- ✓ Be happy.
- ✓ Laugh a lot, but with good support.
- ✓ Avoid stress.
- ✓ Avoid places with foul air. Everything you breathe passes through your voice instrument.
- ✓ Inhale at the belly (like an inner tube around your waist) and relax the belly to exhale (i.e., let your belly hang out, "feel fat").
- ✓ Eat well.
- ✓ Avoid dairy products prior to extensive speaking because they produce mucus.
- ✓ Treat your body like a priceless instrument.
- ✓ Humidify your bedroom during winter months.
- ✓ Drink lots of water, about eight glasses a day, to avoid dehydration.

THE ART OF LISTENING

Listening is an art that when done well delivers tremendous benefits. The goal of listening well is to achieve win-win communication. Win-win communication not only fosters understanding, affirmation, validation, and appreciation, but it also creates an atmosphere of trust, honor, and respect. When someone truly listens to you, don't you feel special? Listening well is a two-way street, and to be effective communicators, we must all listen well to each other. One-way listening can be equated to driving down a one-way street the wrong way. It's dangerous, it can get you into trouble, and it can be expensive, as illustrated in the following example.

Sam, a dispatcher for a national moving company in Philadelphia, gave Mike, a new driver, an assignment to go to Portsmouth to make a household goods delivery. When Mike arrived in Portsmouth, he called Sam for further instructions. As Sam gave Mike the necessary information, Mike got a strange feeling that something wasn't quite right. Mike asked Sam for the complete address, which was Maple Street in Portsmouth, Virginia. Well, Mike was in Portsmouth, but it was Portsmouth, Rhode Island. Mike was ten hours away from where he was supposed to be. He had traveled north in the wrong direction. Not only did this cost the company time and money, but also the owner of the goods was not pleased. What caused this expensive mistake? Ineffective listening by both parties. In his haste, Mike didn't listen to all the information that Sam gave him, and Sam neglected to get accurate acknowledgment from Mike stating that he understood the instructions.

Focus on the Caller

Listening well is a skill that requires practice. Someone who listens well easily establishes rapport with others. Good listeners attract others because they focus on the speaker completely. They have a positive energy that makes you want to be in their company. They are effective in their jobs because, by listening and asking the appropriate questions, they know exactly what needs to be done and how to do it.

To be effective when interacting over the telephone, hone your verbal skills and focus completely on what the speaker is saying. Listen closely to your intuition. The best example of this is to observe how blind people communicate. Since they do not have the gift of sight, they focus on their other gifts and develop them. Their hearing is acute, and they can "people read" by focusing on a person's voice attitude and the words that the person uses. Those of us whose work depends on the telephone should do the same. A good listener, both on the telephone and in person, will:

- Always be prepared to take notes when necessary. That means having writing tools readily available.

- Repeat the information he or she heard by saying, "I hear you saying...Is that correct?" If the speaker does not agree, repeat the process to ensure understanding.

- Remain curious and ask questions to determine if he or she is accurately understanding the speaker.

- Want to listen to the information being delivered.

- Be physically and mentally present in the moment.

- Listen by using the ears to "hear" the message, the eyes to "read" body language (when listening in person), the mind to visualize the person speaking (when on the telephone), and intuition to determine what the speaker is actually saying.

- Establish rapport by "following the leader." Match the momentum, tone of voice, body language, and words used by the speaker. Please use common sense when matching. If the speaker is yelling, don't do the same because it will make a bad situation worse.

A poor listener, both on the telephone and in person:

- May be abrupt and/or give one word answers such as "no," "yes," and "maybe."

- Will be easily distracted. In person, the listener may look around the room as opposed to focusing on the speaker's face. Over the telephone, the listener may be opening mail, reading e-mail, filing, playing with hair, a pencil, or a tie—anything that preempts focusing on the caller.

■ Constantly interrupts, making the speaker feel that what he or she has to say is not important. The listener finishes the other person's sentences, implying that the listener already knows what the speaker is about to say.

■ Changes the subject without even realizing it.

■ Looks at his watch, signaling that you are wasting his time.

Remember that effective listening can open many doors. If you listen with your eyes, your ears, and your mind, you will always get the information you need.

DISCOVERING YOUR CUSTOMER'S STYLE

Now that we have talked about voice tone, volume, timbre, pitch, speed, and listening, it's time to combine all these ingredients with a method of communication that will help you serve your customer better over the telephone.

Most of us believe in the Golden Rule, "Do unto others as you would have them do unto you." Doesn't everyone want to be treated the way you want to be treated? I think not. Tony Alessandra, Ph.D. puts a different spin on the Golden Rule and calls the new version the "Platinum Rule." It reads, "Do unto others as they would like to be done unto." Doesn't that make more sense? By understanding the person with whom you are communicating, you can give them what they want in the manner that they want it. It's so simple, yet so difficult, because adapting and changing to another person's style takes practice, understanding, and flexibility. Most of us expect others to adapt to our standards, yet we often exclude ourselves from the same process.

Unfortunately, this does little to open the lines of communication. By learning to listen carefully with your eyes, ears, and mind, and also by using a special language known as DISC, you can identify the other person's communication style and deliver your information accordingly.

The DISC acronym represents four styles of observable behaviors: Dominant, Influential, Steady, and Conscientious. The dominant style directs everyone. The influential style is a master socializer. The steady style loves relating to people. The conscientious style is the thinker of the group. Most people are a combination of all four of these styles, and their behavior may change from environment to environment. To further illustrate this concept, think of how your behavior differs at home, at work, and at play.

The DISC language has been in existence since people began watching other people. Over time, this language has had many different names. It is a language that focuses on verbal, vocal, and visual cues. Have you ever sat in a mall, airport, railroad, or bus station and just watched people? Individual styles of acting and speaking tell us so much about a person. It's fun sitting back and observing the wide variety of behavior in this diverse world of ours. Yet the similarities among us span all cultures and can be easily categorized into four groups. Some people are open, friendly, and talkative, while others are more reserved and quiet. Some people are more task-oriented, whereas others are more people-oriented. These cues are the keys of the DISC communication language. Learning how to interpret the cues, and adapting your personal style to them, will enhance your ability to communicate with everyone you meet.

To describe the individual characteristics of the four DISC styles, meet some interesting people: **D**ominique Director, **I**vana Extravert, **S**teadman Empathizer, and **C**onrad Analyzer.

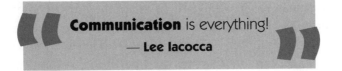

Communication is everything!
— **Lee Iacocca**

Each of these individuals is special. Remember them well because you will be meeting them over and over again—in person, on the telephone, and in many other places.

Dominique Director

The Dominant Director

(adapted from "The High D" by Randy Widrick, TTI International, Ltd.)

Dominique Director, the driver, the "D"
Unconquerable, demanding, aggressive, free
Brave, decisive, competitive, tough
Up to the task, direct, sometimes rough!

Quick to the draw, flip with the lip
You'll get it direct, straight from the hip
She'll climb any mountain, nothing's too high
She aims to succeed, whatever she tries!

Results are the focus, press on to new heights
Along the way, expect a few fights
Don't take it personal, she just speaks her mind,
So pick up the pace, or get left behind!

You may smirk a little when you hear her rant
Of all that she'll win if her wish you grant
Give her a challenge that's brave and bold
Stand back and watch as she "brings home the gold!"

As you can see, Dominique is a powerhouse. With a name like Dominique Director, you can bet that she loves challenge, change, and being in control. Her pace is quick and results oriented as she focuses on her goal with a no-nonsense energy. Fiercely independent and competitive, Dominique is all business. Wasting time makes her impatient. She'll break rules when necessary to achieve her goals and beg for forgiveness afterward. Ask her to take on a project, and she takes the ball and runs with nary a second thought. When you speak with her, get to the point quickly before she gets bored, and don't be taken aback by her bluntness. When selling a product or service, focus on what the product does, what it will do for her, and the cost.

Use some of these phrases and words when communicating with the Dominiques in your world: **win, be the best or first, benefits, now, control, results, challenge, fast, today, quick, lead the field, bottom line, immediate, new and unique, saves time.**

Some dos and don'ts when communicating with Dominique both in person and over the telephone:

DON'T

✓ Ramble on and waste time.

✓ Try to build personal relationships.

✓ Chitchat or ask personal questions.

✓ Be unprepared or disorganized.

✓ Leave loopholes or cloudy issues.

✓ Force Dominique into a losing situation.

✓ Ask rhetorical or unnecessary questions.

✓ Expect to take your time making decisions.

✓ Make the decision for her. She needs the control.

✓ Take issue with Dominique personally.

DO

- ✓ Be clear and specific.
- ✓ Stick to business.
- ✓ Get to the point.
- ✓ Be prepared, organized, and know material well.
- ✓ Present facts logically, professionally, and efficiently. Establish goals and boundaries.
- ✓ Ask specific "what" questions.
- ✓ Make decisions quickly.
- ✓ Give her control by providing alternatives and choices for her to make decisions.
- ✓ Take issue with the facts, when disagreeing.
- ✓ Provide a win-win opportunity.

When calling Dominique, always ask if it's a good time to speak. Interruptions bother her as she is focused and moves quickly. Note that she has a direct tone of voice and speaks in a strong, clear, and confident manner. Dominique enjoys new and unique products and services that save time and money, are effective, and provide results. Be prepared for Dominique to ask "what" questions: "What will this training do for my company?" "What will this training provide for my people?" "What is the cost of this program?" Follow up after the sale with proof of the results.

When Dominique calls you, she may begin speaking without identifying herself. She'll barrel right down to business without any concern for what you are doing. Her tone of voice will be direct and straightforward. Even before she speaks, you can sense the direct energy coming through the receiver.

Famous people who share Dominique's behavior style are Hillary Clinton, Barbara Walters, Roseanne Barr,

Madonna, John McEnroe, Sam Donaldson, Fidel Castro, Rush Limbaugh, and Michael Jordan.

Ivana Extravert

The Influential Extravert

(adapted from "The High I" by Randy Widrick, TTI International, Ltd.)

> Influencer, expressive, sanguine, the "I"
> Life's full of hope, the limit's the sky
> Enthusiastic, fun, trusting, charming
> Confident, optimistic, popular, disarming.
>
> Words, smooth as cream as she talks to you
> Winning you over to her point of view
> A sparkling eye, a smile that's bright
> In the dark of night, Ivana sees the light.
>
> A people person with a need to be liked
> Inspiring the team to continue the fight
> Talking a lot while getting work done
> Don't worry a bit, work should be fun.
>
> A joke or two, expect a high five
> Ivana adds humor, keeps things alive
> Turn her loose and watch what's done
> The team is inspired to work as ONE.

Ivana Extravert loves people and needs them to like her. Rarely alone and often the center of attention, she is a whirlwind with open gestures and smiles for all. Change often passes by her without any effect. Her speech is animated, and her tone of voice has energy and enthusiasm. Assign her a project and she will take it on with gusto—until she loses interest. She'll be aware of rules, but may break them unintentionally to accomplish her goals. Check to make sure Ivana gets the project done because she doesn't always finish what she starts. Lateness may come with the territory when dealing with Ivana, so plan ahead when making appointments with her.

When speaking with Ivana, be prepared to spend time chitchatting, with you doing the listening. Ever the talker, the gift of persuasion belongs to her, and she is adept at using it to her advantage. Ivana wears her heart on her sleeve and sometimes trusts too deeply. This can put her in a position where she may be taken advantage of. She is intuitive and trusts her "gut" feelings. Organization and planning are not her strengths. Consequently, she may be short on follow-through, waste time, and occasionally appear unprofessional. Ivana enjoys showy products and buys on impulse, taking risks from time to time.

Some phrases and words that you can use when communicating with the Ivanas in your world: **fun, you will look great, tons of people, may I have your opinion, feel, recognition, picture this, testimonials, exciting, put you in the spotlight, freedom, how are you?**

Consider some dos and don'ts when communicating with Ivana both in person and over the telephone.

DON'T

✓ Legislate or muffle.

✓ Be curt, cold, or tight-lipped.

✓ Focus on facts, figures, and alternatives.

✓ Leave decisions up in the air.

✓ Be impersonal or task oriented.

✓ Waste time in "dreaming."

✓ Cut the meeting short or be too businesslike.

✓ Take too much time. Get to action items.

DO

✓ Support her dreams and intentions.

✓ Allow time for relating and socializing.

✓ Talk about people and their goals.

✓ Focus on people and action items. Put details in writing.

✓ Ask for her opinion.

✓ Provide ideas for implementing action.

✓ Be stimulating, fun, and fast moving.

✓ Provide testimonials from important people.

✓ Offer special, immediate, and extra incentives for her willingness to take risks.

When calling Ivana, prepare to spend time socializing before getting down to business. Expressive and energetic describes her energy well. Her tone of voice is colorful, uplifting, and always pleasant. When she answers the phone, ask if it's a good time to speak. She will be most impressed by your manners. Prepare for "who" questions when selling your product or service. Typical questions may be: "Who already buys this product?" "Who else do you deliver this training program to?" "Who will be my contact person?" As long as the product or service makes her look good, she will be happy.

When Ivana calls you, you can sense her expressive, positive energy before you state your greeting. You will either groan, knowing she is talkative and you have little time to speak, or you'll smile because she is so much fun. We all need humor in our lives, and she can provide it.

Famous people who share Ivana's behavior style are President Bill Clinton, Robin Williams, Arnold Palmer, Bette Midler, Tony Danza, Oprah Winfrey, Carol Burnett, Eddie Murphy, and Magic Johnson.

Steadman Empathizer

The Steady Empathizer

(adapted from the High "S" by Randy Widrick, TTI International, Ltd.)

The steady relater, amiable, Steadman
Mild, laid back, patient, no stress
Stable, sincere, passive, serene
Great listening skills, an "ace" on the team.

Hard at work behind the scenes
Helping to do what's best for the team
Others will tire, but Steadman will finish
Determined to stay 'til the task has diminished.

Loyal, devoted, Steadman'll be here awhile
Jumping around just isn't his style
Won't leave a job until it is over
Finish one first, he's not a rover.

Acutely aware of people's needs
Responding to personal hurts on the team
Although appearing slow in the jobs "S's" do
When it comes to a team, Steadman's the "glue."

This poem clearly paints Steadman as a team player and peacekeeper. As his name indicates, Steadman is as steady as they come, with an informal, relaxed, and thoughtful pace. He is an introverted person for whom change comes hard. He likes to maintain the status quo. His patient, soft-spoken, non-expressive style expertly masks deep emotions that he keeps to himself. Fiercely loyal and trustworthy, his personal and work relationships are usually long-term. Trusting takes time for Steadman, and he keeps you at arm's length until he's comfortable. Steadman's gift of listening makes him powerful, but he doesn't perceive himself this way and prefers to be in the background. He serves others not out of necessity or political gain, but because he genuinely enjoys it.

At work Steadman is somewhat systematic and may be a list maker. He doesn't take risks and tends to follow rules. He enjoys finishing one task at a time because when he tries to juggle several tasks, Steadman becomes quite stressed.

Let's look at some phrases and words that you can use when communicating with the Steadmans in your world: **think about it, logical, step by step, promise, work together, take your time, trust me, security, help you out, no rush, guarantee, slowly, help me out.**

Some dos and don'ts when communicating with Steadman both in person and over the telephone:

DON'T

✓ Rush headlong into business or the agenda.

✓ Stick coldly or harshly to business.

✓ Force Steadman into a quick decision or response to your goals.

✓ Threaten or demand.

✓ Promise what you can't deliver.

✓ Interrupt as Steadman speaks (making it appear that you are not listening).

✓ Move quickly and abruptly.

✓ Assume that you have Steadman's "buy-in" due to his willingness to follow your plans and goal.

DO

- ✓ Patiently draw out his goals and ideas, and listen well to Steadman by being responsive.
- ✓ Make your presentation in a logical, soft-spoken manner.
- ✓ Listen well and ask specific "how" questions.
- ✓ Move casually and informally.
- ✓ Show sincere interest in Steadman as a person.
- ✓ Look and listen for hurt feelings if the situation impacts Steadman personally.
- ✓ Provide personal assurances and guarantees.
- ✓ Allow time for Steadman to think.

When calling Steadman, ask if it is a good time to speak. Listen carefully because he is so tolerant that he may not say that it's an inconvenient time. Steadman welcomes your call with a gentle, warm tone of voice and friendly air of concern. When presenting a product or service, explain clearly how it will benefit him. Explain in detail what changes would need to be made if he uses your service or product.

When Steadman calls you, you may sense a calmness as you answer the telephone. His soothing voice tone comes across steady and secure. If he appears wishy-washy when making a decision, give him time to think and offer to call him back when convenient for him. Steadman's questions will focus on how your product or service will benefit and affect himself, his coworkers, and his employees.

Famous people who share Steadman's behavior style are John Denver, Michael J. Fox, Tom Brokaw, Ted Danson, Mr. Rogers, Mother Teresa, Barbara Bush, and Gandhi.

Conrad Analyzer

The Conscientious Analyzer

(adapted from the High "C" by Randy Widrick, TTI International, Ltd.)

Compliant, analytical, melancholic, the "C"
Methodical, courteous, complete accuracy
Restrained, diplomatic, mature, and precise
Accurate, systematic, those standards are nice.

Planning and organizing done to perfection
The smallest detail is no exception
Consistently clear and objective thinking
Gives the team top-notch results without blinking.

And when it comes time to make a decision
You'd best have the facts to accomplish the mission
Conrad at your side with all the correct facts
Will assure the return on your investment won't lack.

Go by the book, follow the rules
Procedures are written, use the right tools
Standards are crucial, both now and later
In God we trust, all other use DATA!

Meticulous, analytical, and perfectionist accurately describe Conrad. His home and office are organized with everything in its place. An unassuming person, Conrad sets high standards and is an example for everyone who works with him. He is skeptical by nature and demands that you have your facts straight. Otherwise, he will shoot holes right through your plans. A private, direct, and unemotional person, Conrad enjoys working in a quiet environment with few people and little noise. He tends to keep people at arm's length and prefers to focus on the task at hand. When selling to Conrad, be aware that he buys slowly. Offer him proven products with lots of information.

Some phrases and words that you can use when communicating with the Conrads in your world: **here are the facts, the data shows, think it over, proven, no risk, analyze, guarantees, take your time, supporting data, "by the book," high standards, high quality.**

The following list contains some dos and don'ts to use when communicating with Conrad both in person and over the telephone:

DON'T   ✓ Be disorganized and messy.

✓ Be casual, informal, or personal.

✓ Force quick decisions.

✓ Be vague about expectations.

✓ Fail to follow through.

✓ Overpromise results. Be conservative.

✓ Behave abruptly and quickly.

✓ Focus on feelings or opinions for support.

✓ Use closing statements.

✓ Try to get close physically or emotionally.

DO   ✓ Prepare in advance and be organized.

✓ Address him formally and directly.

✓ Look at all sides of an issue, approach thoughtfully, and provide the time needed for a decision.

✓ Set definite goals.

✓ Provide follow-through.

✓ Draw an action plan with scheduled dates and milestones.

✓ Take your time, but be persistent.

✓ Use facts, data, or testimonials when disagreeing.

✓ Use incentives.

✓ Allow him space.

Be well prepared before calling Conrad. When you make the call, identify yourself and ask if it's a good time to speak. Because he is the formal type, do not address him by his first name. Speak in a direct, slow, and accurate manner with little variation in your voice. State your reason for calling, avoiding chitchat and personal conversation. Conrad may be a man of few words, so his silence may indicate that he is thinking.

When Conrad calls, you will notice that he is direct with his questions and sounds unemotional. His tone of voice says "no-nonsense," but in a slow manner. Conrad focuses on collecting information before making decisions, so he will ask "why" questions: "Why will this work for me?" "Why should I buy this product?"

Famous people and characters who share Conrad's behavior style are Diane Sawyer, Kevin Costner, Chris Evert, Ted Koppel, Mr. Spock, Monica Seles, Jack Nicklaus, Barbara Stanwyck, and Felix Unger.

PUTTING IT ALL TOGETHER

Now that you have met Dominique, Ivana, Steadman, and Conrad, you should have an understanding of the four behavior styles. Don't forget that we are a combination of all four styles and that our behaviors change according to our environment. When on the telephone, ask yourself these questions to help you identify the style of the other person:

- Do you sense his or her energy as cool or warm?

- Does the person seem fast-paced or slow-paced?

- Is the tone of voice direct or indirect?

- Is the voice volume high, low, loud, or soft?

- Is the person's speech animated, friendly, unemotional, or self-assured?

- Is the person impatient, attentive, receptive, or responsive when listening?

By asking yourself these questions, you will be able to communicate more effectively with the person on the other end of the telephone line.

This chapter just touches the surface of the DISC communication language. Like any other language, it needs to be practiced in order to use it well. Taking a course in DISC will help you identify your own behavior style and give you further information on identifying the behavioral styles of others.

The following tables give you a quick overview of the four behavior styles discussed in this chapter and their characteristics. Choose the table that works best for you. Keep them close to your phone for quick reference.

Table 2.1 DISC and the Four Character Types

DISC	Dominique Director	Ivana Extravert	Steadman Empathizer	Conrad Analyzer
Tone of Voice	Direct	Enthusiastic	Friendly	Direct
Energy	Cool	Warm	Warm	Cool
Pace	Fast Commanding	Fast Impulsive	Slow Calm	Slow Methodical
Speech	Self-assured Controls dialogue	Animated Lively	Friendly Soft spoken	Unemotional No small talk
Listening	Impatient Quick answers	Responsive Interjects often	Receptive Focused	Attentive Analyzing
Goals	Results Control	Recognition People	Security Stability	Accuracy Order
Questions	When	Who	How	Why
Responds to	Options Efficiency	Testimonials Saving effort	Stability Service	Quality Accuracy Logic
Decision Style	Quick	Emotional (gut feel)	Deliberate	Analytical
Follow Up Letter	Bottom line Direct Bullets	Short Personal Friendly	Personal Friendly Assurances	Organized Details Facts

DISC information courtesy of TTI International Ltd., Scottsdale, Arizona

Table 2.2 Tele-DISC

Tele-DISC

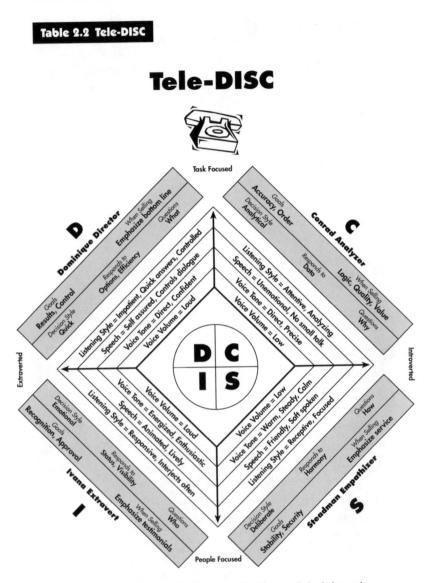

Start from the center and work out to help you identify your caller's telephone style.
© *1998 Image Plus . . .® Associates*

CHAPTER THREE

Don't Hang Up On Opportunity: Telephone Manners Make a Difference

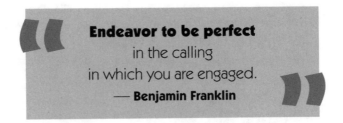

Endeavor to be perfect
in the calling
in which you are engaged.
— **Benjamin Franklin**

Mr. Franklin didn't have telephone skills in mind when he made the above statement, but it's certainly applicable. Whether you work at a Fortune 500 company or a Small Office Home Office (SOHO), your telephone skills are important to business and career success. Look at what business people had to say in a survey done by *Communications Briefings* of Alexandria, VA.

How much does the way the phone is answered influence your opinion of the company you are calling?

- 82% — A lot
- 17% — Some
- 1% — Not much

Which of the following company phone practices bothers you the most?

- 42% — Automated phone menus
- 25% — Not answering by the third or fourth ring
- 21% — Toll numbers that are always busy
- 7% — Playing music or ads while you wait
- 5% — Other. This choice included such practices as no answering machines after hours, no etiquette for the timely return of calls, and no policy for placing someone on hold.

From our clients to our coworkers, from the mailroom to the boardroom, we use the telephone to sell our ideas and ourselves and to provide customer service. Everyone in an organization—whether it be a business, educational institution, or government agency—answers the telephone or places a call at one time or another. It's a piece of cake! You pick up the receiver and dial or press a few numbers and talk into the receiver. It's so easy that employers often assume that the people they hire already know how to use the telephone. Or do they?

People are sometimes afraid to use the phone. Why? Because they believe that:

- **They are a bother.** Making and receiving phone calls are a part of doing business. It's expected.

- **They are intruding on someone's valuable time.** Time is money. If you can save someone time with your product or service, you're saving them money. If you need questions answered or need help, and you don't pick up the phone to ask for it, you are wasting your own valuable time. Also, you are not allowing others the opportunity to listen to you or help you out.

- **They don't know what to say when answering or making a call.** That's what this chapter's all about. You'll learn how to do both quickly, politely, and efficiently.

EXECUTIVE TELEPHONE MANNERS

How many executives do you know who answer the telephone well or take a good message? Do you know any that can transfer a call without losing the caller? If you are an executive and you can do these things, then you deserve a pat on the back.

In my image courses, I advise employees to observe how their managers dress and behave. Think about it. If your boss wears professional business clothing, you certainly shouldn't wear sweats to the office. Likewise, you should answer the telephone the way your boss does. But what happens when your boss's telephone skills are poor or nonexistent? Executives sometimes forget that, as leaders, they set the example. An executive with good telephone manners sets a powerful example because employees tend to emulate their bosses.

If you are an executive, you may be saying, "It doesn't matter because my secretary answers my phone." Oh, really? Your secretary may answer the call, but to whom does she transfer the call? So executives, listen up! Don't expect your people to have great telephone manners if you don't have them yourself. Use the phone well and they will, too. Poor telephone manners delivered by an executive reflects badly on an organization. How you speak to people, whether in person or over the phone, says a lot about you and your company.

Recently my associate answered our business phone and heard a gruff voice ask, "Is Ana there?" My associate responded that I was out of the office and asked if he could help him or take a message. The caller responded in a negative tone with, "I'll call back," and hung up. My friends and colleagues call me Terry, which is short for Ana Teresa. Obviously, this person was not a long-term friend of mine.

Mr. Gruff called back twice when I was not available and delivered the same "I'll call back" message in the same negative tone. Not leaving a message or identifying himself was becoming irritating to me, especially since he refused to allow anyone else to help him. If he had left a phone number, I would have gladly called him back. Finally, he called when I was available. The moment he spoke, I knew it was Mr. Gruff, and I sat back and listened to his sales pitch with amazement.

The organization that Mr. Gruff represented had sent materials to me earlier in the week. The package gave a positive first impression that piqued my interest. Mr. Gruff told me that he believed in this organization so much that he came out of retirement to take over as vice president of membership and to handle the company's financing. I thought, "Vice President! Financing! You've got to be kidding me! How can this person hold such a title yet represent his organization so poorly over the phone?"

Mr. Gruff had a harsh style and spoke to me in a condescending manner. He told me that he had been in business for twenty years. In addition, he worked for a government program that provided help to entrepreneurs. Again, I asked myself how this person could be in business for twenty years with telephone skills such as these. He certainly didn't set a positive example.

Unfortunately, no one ever taught Mr. Gruff how to use the telephone properly. This executive delivered a poor impression of the organization he was representing, and he lost credibility with his first call. Additional credibility was lost with each subsequent call. By the time he reached me, I was not interested in what he had to say. The only reason I listened as long as I did was because the company's written materials were so impressive. The lack of congruency between the materials Mr. Gruff sent and his telephone manners waved a big red flag at me. Did he make the sale? Of course not! To make matters worse, on his last call he asked me, "Where do we stand now, dear?" Right.

Presenting 4C Image Telephone Manners

Poor manners really stand out, and some are most annoying! Review the following tips carefully because they really can make a difference.

- Don't chew gum while talking on the telephone. Calls are intended for people, not cows.

- Don't eat or drink while on the phone. That crunchy

pickle, crisp apple, and hard Bavarian pretzel are best eaten when you are not talking on the phone. No one needs to know your diet.

■ Remember to say please, thank you, and you're welcome. In today's society, those words are becoming a rarity. We need to bring them back into the mainstream.

■ Don't open mail, read a report, or write a letter when on the phone. Give the person on the line your undivided attention.

■ Don't answer the phone when you are in a meeting. Either turn on your voice mail or have a secretary or receptionist take your calls. If you must take a call, inform the participants before the meeting starts.

■ If someone's on a call, don't interrupt her. Either leave a message on her desk or return at another time.

■ Put the caller on hold before discussing his problem or situation with a coworker. It's embarrassing to have the caller hear something confidential or unkind said about him or someone else.

■ Driving and cell phones don't mix. If you must use your cell phone, pull over to the side of the road.

■ Do not talk on your cell phone at the dinner table in a restaurant. It looks pretentious, and it's rude.

■ Always treat others with trust, honor, and respect. It can be sensed when interacting over the telephone.

TYPES OF CALLS

Whether in person or over the phone, customers need to know and feel that they are at the center of your attention when they interact with you. Different types of customers require different approaches. Knowing how to manage the call will help you get what you want, whether selling a product or a service, making an appointment, requesting information, or handling complaints. Calls are broken down into three categories:

- **Inbound**—Calls coming into a business
- **Outbound**—Calls going out of a business
- **In-house**—Interdepartmental calls

In all three categories you will be engaged in a mixed bag of sales and customer service. When you hear the words "sales" or "customer service," different images may enter your mind. To some, the word "sales" presents challenges and opportunities to provide products or services that enhance customers' lives. To others, that same word may create discomfort, because they see someone pressuring them to purchase products or services they don't want or need. The words "customer service" may be equated with fixing problems, providing service, and making people happy. Yet to others, those same words create a mental picture of a person sitting behind a desk pulling his hair out from listening to complaints. As with everything, interpretation is in the mind of the listener.

Inbound Calls

Answering the Call

The first few seconds of a telephone call set the tone for your conversation, and how you answer the phone certainly influences that interaction. Every person who calls your workplace should hear a 4C Image greeting.

Avoid answering the phone too quickly. Picking up on the first ring gives the impression that you are just sitting there waiting for the phone to ring—almost like a sign of desperation. Answering between the second and third ring is a good rule of thumb to follow. By the fourth ring, the caller becomes impatient and the organization begins to appear unprofessional, so don't let it go beyond that if possible.

Provide sufficient information. Answering a business phone with a simple hello or the name of the department—for example, sales—does not deliver enough information to the caller. Without proper information, there's no direction and the caller feels he's in the middle of an intersection not knowing which road to take.

Answer the call with a strong greeting. Like a handshake when first meeting someone, the words and tone of voice used when answering the telephone set the stage for the interaction. A weak greeting, like a weak handshake, may give a wishy-washy impression of the company and of the person answering the call. A strong greeting, like a strong handshake, delivers a sense of power and control that leads to a 4C Image. By using welcoming phrases such as good morning, good afternoon, good evening, or thank you for calling, you "extend your hand" and help the caller feel comfortable. The beginnings of a positive connection have been created.

State your company name and personal name. Continue strengthening the connection by stating your company name and/or, depending on the situation, your personal name after the welcoming phrase. Adding your name helps the caller to connect with you and makes it easier for him to tell you why he is calling. Depending on your environment, using first names may be acceptable. In a more formal environment, using first and last names are appropriate when answering the phone.

Ask the caller how you can help him or her. Lastly, lead the caller into telling you what he wants by simply asking him. Use a phrase appropriate to your place of business such as, "How may I help you?" or "How may I direct your call?"

Put it all together and this is what you have:

Good morning, Smelly International, Juan speaking. How may I help you? or *How may I direct your call?*

Smile and sound sincere. When you say your greeting, mean it! Put a smile on your face. Let the person on the other end believe that you are ecstatic he is calling. Drop what you are doing and give him your undivided attention. Look into a mirror before you pick up the phone to make sure that your facial expressions are warm and friendly. Refer to Chapter 4 for more information on the use of mirrors with the telephone.

Avoid shortcuts. Have you ever experienced those days when the workplace becomes so harried that it's difficult to remember the time of day? Answering the phone by just saying the company name or your name becomes ever so tempting. Avoid it. You never know if the person calling could be your next big account, so don't settle for anything less than a 4C Image greeting. When things get crazy in the workplace, shorten the greeting by eliminating the welcoming phrase.

Ding Dong Corporation, Nancy Curlicue speaking. May I help you?

Be carefully creative with your greeting. A friend of mine, a chiropractor, trains his employees to answer the phone with this energetic greeting:

It's a great day at Happy Back Chiropractic! This is _____. How may I help you?

When I first heard this greeting, it took me aback. At first it seemed corny, but I later realized there was a smile on my face every time I hung up from making an appointment. The positive energy that flowed from beginning to end of that call was undeniable. Interestingly enough, that same energy always met me at the door when I went to the office for my appointment.

Take caution with your creativity, however. Some greetings, especially those left on answering machines, may be funny or entertaining to you, but not to your caller. If in doubt, run it past several people and get their opinions. More on answering machine greetings later in this chapter.

Remember: Answering the telephone with a pleasant greeting, identifying yourself and your company, and then asking the caller how you can help him or her are the pathways that connect you with your caller.

Hold On, Please!

Hold on, please...those dreaded words! It's annoying and rude to be placed in a perpetual holding pattern before you can state why you are calling, especially if you're calling long-distance. Being forced to listen to silence (making you wonder if you've been disconnected) or to distracting music is not amusing. It's assumed that you're able to hold. Bad assumption! You may have just lost a client.

A workplace necessity, the hold button has carved out its own special place on the list of indispensable telephone features. It's a true love/hate relationship that you can't live with or without, and it should be used as sparingly as possible. So let's learn how to tame this little beast so that we can all live with it more comfortably.

Few people like to be told what to do. When you tell someone to please hold or hold on or hold on a minute, you are giving that person a command. Any positive connection you may have established dissipates in an instant. Instead of giving the caller a command, give her a choice by asking permission. These two little phrases—*Can you please hold?* or *May I put you on hold, please?*—show respect for the caller and her time and allow her to tell you what works for her. Let's take a look at the following example:

> **Operator:** *Accurate Accounting.*
>
> **Mari:** *Uh, hello, this is Mari Starlite. I would like to speak with Charlie Tuna in* (operator cuts her off).
>
> **Operator:** *Hold, please.*

In this scenario, the operator comes across coolly, and rudely interrupts Mari. Mari Starlight has no way to connect mentally or emotionally with the receptionist. No 4C Image here. Let's take a look at what happens when the operator changes his approach.

> **Receptionist:** *Good morning, Accurate Accounting, this is Dave, how may I help you?*
>
> **Mari:** *Hello, Dave. This is Mari Starlite. I would like to speak with Charlie Tuna in sales, please.*
>
> **Receptionist:** *May I put you on hold while I transfer your call, Ms. Starlight?*
>
> **Mari:** *Of course. Thank you.*

Now that's 4C Image material. Dave created a positive connection by introducing himself and his company and asking how he could help the caller. He further addressed Mari properly and asked for permission to put her on hold before he transferred her.

Let's take this call one step further, when the call can't be transferred right away:

> **Receptionist:** *Thank you for holding, Ms. Starlite. Mr. Tuna is on another line. Would you care to continue holding, leave a message on Mr. Tuna's voice mail, or could someone else in sales help you?*
>
> **Mari:** *I'll leave a message on Mr. Tuna's voice mail.*

> **Receptionist:** *For future reference, Mr. Tuna's direct line with voice mail is 555-0000. I will now transfer you.*
>
> **Mari:** *Thank you.*

The first positive step Dave took was to thank Mari for holding. Then he gave Mari the opportunity to make a choice of speaking with another sales agent or leaving voice mail. Additionally, he offered Mary Mr. Tuna's direct line. The positive connection continues, and the call closes on an up note. If the person answering the call had been Mr. Tuna's administrative assistant or a fellow sales associate, the interaction could have gone like this:

> **Assistant:** *Good morning, Accurate Accounting, this is Dave, how may I help you?*
>
> **Mari:** *Hello, Dave. This is Mari Starlight. I would like to speak with Charlie Tuna in sales, please.*
>
> **Assistant:** *Mr. Tuna is not available at the moment, Ms. Starlite. I'm Charlie's assistant. May I help you?*
>
> **Mari:** *Of course. Thank you.*

Taking Messages

The art of message taking escapes many of us. Clear, concise messages save time, energy, and miscommunication. The following key points will guide you through the process to help you create those positive interactions.

Keep a writing pad and pen or pencil close at hand. It appears unprofessional to hunt for paper and pen as the caller listens to you opening drawers and rustling papers. Keep these materials in an accessible spot. Use message pads with carbons so that you have a copy of the message in the event it gets misplaced. You can place a sticky note in an obvious place on a person's desk.

Ask for the caller's name. Do not react to difficult or strange sounding names. A comment such as *that's a strange name* or *that's a funny spelling* is rude and may be offensive to the caller. Yes, there are times when you may have to bite your tongue, but remember that a name is the one thing we really own in this life. You may lose all your material wealth, but you'll still have your name.

Ask for the correct spelling of the name and listen carefully. Repeat back the spelling to make sure that you heard it correctly. After clearly spelling my name, people still write what they think they hear. I consistently receive information with my named spelled Terri Wilderman instead of Terry Wildemann.

Use the caller's name throughout the interaction. If the caller uses both first and last names, address him by his last name. If the caller wants to be addressed by his first name, let him tell you so. Don't assume. This shows respect and personalizes the call. Some people find it offensive to have strangers call them by their first names.

Ask for the person's area code, telephone number, and extension. Some people may say, "Oh, he has my number." *Kindly insist* on taking it down anyway. This technique saves valuable time by avoiding the need to look up the caller's phone number later. It's especially helpful for the traveler who calls in for messages to have all the information delivered at once.

Ask for a message. Write the message clearly and accurately. The recipient of the message should not have to come back to you to clarify what you wrote.

Repeat the message to the caller to make sure you wrote it down correctly.

Ask for the best time to return the call. The recipient can call back when it's convenient for both parties, and they can both pay full attention to the call.

Write down the time and date of the call. This information can be used later if necessary.

The following example highlights the above steps:

> **Assistant:** *Mr. Tuna is not available at the moment, Ms. Starlite. I'm Charlie's assistant. May I help you?*
>
> **Mari:** *Please call me Mari. I would like to speak with Mr. Tuna directly, but since he's not available, may I leave a message with you?*
>
> **Assistant:** *Of course, Mari. Do you spell Mari with a* y *or an* i*?*
>
> **Mari:** *With an* i.
>
> **Assistant:** *Could you please spell your last name, Mari?*
>
> **Mari:** *That's* s-t-a-r-l-i-t-e.
>
> **Assistant:** *OK, Mari, may I have your phone number, please?*
>
> **Mari:** *123-456-7890.*
>
> **Assistant:** *That's 123-456-7890.*
>
> **Mari:** *Correct.*
>
> **Assistant:** *And your message?*
>
> **Mari:** *I'm calling in response to his letter of June 13, 1998. Please return my call.*
>
> **Assistant:** *When would be a convenient time to call, Mari?*
>
> **Mari:** *I'll be in the office until 3 p.m. today and also tomorrow morning.*

Assistant: *Your message should read that you called in reference to his June 13th letter and to please return your call. You will be in until 3 p.m. today and tomorrow morning. Is this correct?*

Mari: *Yes, thanks.*

Assistant: *I'll make sure that he gets the message. Enjoy the day, Mari!*

Outbound Calls

Be Prepared

Rarely does a business day go by without taking a call from someone selling a product or service. After all, without sales how can business survive? When the customer service or sales agent really knows what she is doing, the call can be enjoyable and mutually beneficial. Unfortunately, those calls don't happen as often as most of us would like.

One afternoon I found myself focusing on a sales representative's inability to handle a call that he had rudely forced upon me. His voice had a monotone quality that sounded robotic but anxious at the same time. As he proceeded to read, pause, and raise his voice on cue, I became embarrassed for the rep. Every few words became stumbling

If the call center industry can't operate in an ethical fashion, and in a manner that benefits the people being called, there will be no future for the industry.
— **Angela Karr, managing editor, TeleProfessional Magazine**

blocks. I thought to myself, "My first grader reads better than this young man!" I wondered if he had read the script before making the call. He was so poorly trained!

A sigh of relief came through loud and clear when the young man finally came to the end of his ordeal. When I asked if he had read the script before he made the call, he became very flustered and said, "This is my first day." I suggested that at his next break he should take the script, read it well, and practice it until he could say each word without stumbling. He sounded so dejected that it was obvious he couldn't wait to get off the call. So, I wished him good luck and hung up.

The embarrassment that this young man experienced was absolutely unnecessary. His employer was responsible for training him to deliver a 4C Image on the telephone. Being put in the line of fire without proper training says a great deal about that company's management. The young man was trying his best, but he had no business making calls. He was not ready. His managers and supervisors forgot about taking care of their most important asset, their employee. What if I had hung up on him? How would the young man have felt? It takes a strong person to put up with constant rejection. No wonder there's a 300 percent turnover in the call center industry!

Making Calls With Respect

It's rude to hang up on someone. On occasion, I've had to eat those words, but at least I hang up nicely. When people call and can't pronounce my name, sound comatose, or act like a long lost friend to sell me something, I lose patience with the intrusion. The fatal mistake comes when the caller begins to rattle off his spiel like an out-of-control locomotive at an inopportune time. It's useless telling him that it's not a good time and to call back later. He continues to talk over me as he reads from a script, at which point I tune him out. My only recourse is to respond, "Thank you for calling, but I'm not interested at the moment," and hang up. The thoughtlessness of not asking if it's a good time to call signals the caller's lack of respect for me.

On the other hand, selling products and services to the public is the telemarketer's job, and she is often frustrated by unnecessary abuse and rudeness. When I get a call from a salesperson or telemarketer who has done a good job, I tell her so, because everyone likes to hear compliments. What's accomplished in this Catch-22? Not much other than frustration all around. So the cycle continues until someone comes up with something different—and they have.

When speaking with telephone sales expert Art Sobczak of Business By Phone, Inc., I told him how I felt about the constant cold calls that I receive in my workday. I explained that salespeople calling do not bother me; after all, it's their job and they may be selling something I need. It's being forced to listen to the spiel without having an option that frustrates me.

He offered a solution that really works. When training sales agents at his Telesales Rep College, Sobczak uses the following fill-in-the-blank template, along with word-and-phrase menus. It's perfect for creating your own generic opening statements. It can be adapted for any industry and type of call. Use the template when making outbound calls and create a win-win situation for all. Be creative and have fun coming up with new ways to present your products and services over the telephone.

Art's Fill-in-the-Blanks Opening Statement Formula

The following statement can be tailored to any kind of business or service:

> *"Hello* _____ *I'm* _____ *with* _____. *I'm calling today because depending on what you're now doing/using/experiencing in the area of* (fill in with your area of specialty) *there's a possibility we might be able to help you* (fill in with minimization verb) *your* (fill in with appropriate undesired noun), *while at the same time* (fill in with maximization verb) *your* (fill in with appropriate desired noun). *If I've caught you at a good time, I'd like to* (fill in with action verb) *your situation to see if this is something* (fill in with appropriate ending phrase)*."*

Use the tables below to fill in the desired verbs, nouns, and phrases that will complete your company's opening statement.

Minimization Verb

save	salvage	free up	costs
consolidate	minimize	decrease	slice
trim problems	sit down on	eliminate	get rid of
annoyance	reduce	lessen work	combine
cut	expense	lower	soften
slash	waste	shrink	modify
effort			

Undesired Noun

trouble	difficulty	restriction	obstacle
time	taxes	burden	labor
bother	inconvenience	charges	hassle
drudgery	paperwork	anxiety	help

Maximization Verb

strengthen	intensify	reinforce	boost
increase	add	maximize	create
enjoy	expand	grow	enhance
build	case		

Desired Noun

profits	sales	dollars	revenue
income	dollars	cash flow	savings
market share	time	productivity	morale
motivation	output	attitude	image
victories			

Action Verb/Phrase

discuss	ask questions about	review
go through	analyze	

Ending Phrase

You'd like more information on . . .
You'd like to discuss that . . .
That would be of value . . .
That would be of interest . . .
That's worth considering . . .
That would work for you . . .

Let's look at some examples using this template:

> "Hello, **Ms. Smile-A-Lot**, I'm **Robyn Hoode**
> with **Merry Men Cleaning Solutions**. I'm
> calling today because, depending on what products
> you're now **using** in your **dry cleaning facility**,
> there's a possibility we might be able to help you
> **reduce** your **labor costs**, while at the same time
> **increase** your **profits**. If I've caught you at a
> good time, I'd like to **discuss** your situation to see
> if this is something **that would work for you**."

*"**Dr. Quest**, this is **Mary Brightmouth** with **Best Dental Products**. We specialize in state-of-the-art dental equipment. Depending on what you are **experiencing** now, there's a possibility we might be able to help you **decrease** your **time spent per patient**, while at the same time **improving** your **service**. If I've caught you at a good time, I'd like to **ask you a few questions** to see if what we have **would be of interest to you**."*

*"Hello, **Sister Jean**, I'm **Tutti Longskirt** with **Our Kids Communications**. My purpose for calling you is quite simple: depending on what you are **experiencing** in the area of **interpersonal communications between the teachers and students** in your school, there's a possibility we can assist you and your staff to **reduce classroom difficulties** while **improving teacher morale**. If I've caught you at a good time, I'd like to **ask a few questions** to see if our **program is worth considering**."*

This five-star formula has all the elements needed for a great opening. Most importantly, it shows respect for the recipient by giving him or her options. Grab that thesaurus and work this formula with words appropriate to your industry until it meets your specific needs. Play with it, then test it on colleagues and friends, then re-edit and retest until you get it just right. Have fun!

Interdepartmental Calls

Take a close look at how your interdepartmental calls are handled and you may be surprised at what you find. Sadly, employees and coworkers take each other for granted and offer little or no respect when interacting over the telephone.

Not exactly a healthy workplace situation. The Johnny Self-Absorbeds in the business world are all too common. Why should we treat our coworkers any differently than our customers? We shouldn't. In the same *Communications Briefings* survey referred to earlier, business people answered the question: Which of the following employee habits bothers you most? Take a look at how they responded…

- 34% — Using the hold button without asking
- 30% — Being uninformed
- 15% — Poor grammar
- 11% — Not identifying themselves
- 6% — Mangling the company name

Do these answers sound much different from what a paying customer might say? Absolutely not.

Think about how you answer your own in-house calls. A manager participating in a customer service program that I presented mentioned in a friendly, off-the-cuff manner that he always answers the in-house line with, "Yeah." Well, I doubt he'll be doing this much longer after the earful he got from his staff. He was surprised at their negative response to how he answered the phone and vowed to change his bad habit.

Answering in-house phones with a greeting such as *Accounting, Molly speaking, how may I help you?* certainly sounds better than *Yeah* or *Accounting*. This is most appropriate for large companies where people may not know each other well.

Small companies with few employees tend to be more casual. Still, respect should not be shortchanged. Always identify yourself when answering a call, and ask for permission to put callers on hold. What appear to be insignificant courtesies go a long way toward improving workplace communications.

Voice Mail

Learning to operate your voice mail efficiently can save time and effort and, most importantly, it keeps you connected with your customers twenty-four hours a day. Read your system's manual to find out how it works; the voice-mail system you have worked with for months may have features you never knew about. When all else fails, read the directions. You will be surprised at the power and flexibility at your fingertips.

Voice-mail Greetings

A good voice-mail greeting should be updated frequently, and it should make the caller feel comfortable. Make sure your greeting contains the following ingredients:

Your name. In a company where there are multiple Alexes, Cathys, Bobs, and Jims, you also should include your last name in your greeting. This way the caller knows she has the correct party. *Hi, this is Jim Balaya.*

The day of the week and the date. *Today is Tuesday, March 21.*

When you will be available. *I'm out of the office this morning and will be in after 1 p.m.*

Ask for the information that you want from the caller. *Your message is important to me, so please leave your name, number, and the best time to return your call, and I'll get back to you as soon as possible.*

Offer an alternate number such as your secretary, receptionist, colleague, or, if available, offer your beeper or cell phone number. *If you need to speak with someone immediately, please press 23 and my colleague Robert will assist you. You can also call my beeper number 555-5555. Looking forward to speaking with you soon!*

Leaving Voice-mail Messages

Playing touch-tone tag is a nuisance, time-wasting, and most unnecessary. Consider the following unproductive and tedious exchange:

> **Creepy Crawler:** *Hey, Spider! This is Creepy. Have to talk with you about an account! Give me a call.*
>
> **Spider Web:** *Hey, Creepy, I'm in the office this afternoon. Give me a call back.*
>
> **Creepy Crawler:** *Hi, Spider. It's Creepy calling again. Sorry I couldn't get back to you yesterday, but I really have to talk with you. Call me when you're in the office.*
>
> **Spider Web:** *O.K. Creepy. I'm here now; where are you?*

Enough! Let's go over some tips to help you save time and leave a good message. Organize your thoughts *before* you pick up the receiver. Any information that the call recipient needs should be at your fingertips. If you are uncomfortable leaving messages, write down what you need to say first so that you don't forget anything.

Identify yourself. *Hi, Spider. This is Creepy Crawler.*

State a brief, detailed message as to why you're calling. This allows the recipient to return your call with the information you need. *The Monarch Butterfly account is scheduled to metamorphose next week, but I need the exact date in order to arrange the time and place with Mr. Bird and Queen Bee.*

State when you need a response and the best time to call back. *Please call me as soon as possible. I'll be in all afternoon.*

Close. *Thanks, Spider.*

Tips and Tricks for Voice Mail

Change the temporary password. When installing a new system, avoid using obvious passwords such as 1234, 5678, or 2222. They're too easy to figure out.

Avoid giving out your password and change it occasionally. Write it down, then put it in a safe place. If it becomes necessary to give out your password, make sure you change it ASAP after the event. For example, you are working with a team member on a project and while you're away on vacation she will need access to information that is in your mailbox. Give her your password, but change it when you return.

Use one password for each mailbox. Most business systems have mailboxes for each telephone extension. Use a different password for the main mailbox and for each extension's mailbox.

Use the # key to bypass calls. When calling someone frequently, you can often bypass the greeting by pressing the # key.

Avoid using speakerphones to leave voice-mail messages. The quality of the voice message is compromised.

Avoid leaving long messages that contain a lot of data. Facts and figures are confusing enough and delivering large quantities over the phone can lead to mistakes. For these types of messages, consider using fax, e-mail, or snail mail.

Avoid having the caller play voice-mail ping-pong. Callers can get frustrated when the voice-mail system bounces them back and forth. Many callers don't realize that most systems bounce them to a live person when they press "0." Tell them they can do so during your greeting.

Streamline menus and options to no more than four selections. Instructions should be short and simple to follow. The KISS method (Keep It Simple, Silly) works well here.

Maintain the same menu format throughout. We tend to remember the last thing we hear, so it's best to state the action first. Secondly, state the corresponding key to press. For example: *For the sales department, press 2; for accounts payable, press 3.*

Give the most important information first. What you consider the most important information may not be what your customer believes is most important. Use your customers' most common questions and answers to guide you.

ASK QUESTIONS!

Asking questions will help you find out what your clients and coworkers want and need from you. Josiane Feigon, owner of Tele-Smart, provides the following tips to lead you on your way to great telephone communications.

- **Ask open-ended questions** so you can get more information. These are the great conversation makers. If you're at a loss figuring out what to say next, or if you want to open up the conversation and really hear what the customer is saying, ask an open-ended question.

- **Paraphrase** to confirm that you're receiving the correct information. This shows the customer that you're listening and that you're empathizing. For example: "If I understand you correctly, you're saying that..." "What I hear you saying is..." "In other words, you're..." "The way you see things is..."

- **Ask precise questions** to understand your customer's true needs and issues. Precise questions also narrow the sales funnel and cut through potential objections. For example: "How, specifically, do you make that decision?" "What exactly is your goal?" "Where precisely do you have accounts?" "In what particular way could this be easier?" "When specifically do you want to do this?"

Asking Precise Questions

Use the following chart to help you remember the types of precise questions to ask.

Current Situation

What are you doing now?
What are you accomplishing with it?
How is it working or being used?

Customer Motivation

What interests you about our service/product?
What do you hear about our service/product?
What motivated you to call?

Competition

Which other vendors are you considering?
Which other solutions are you considering?
What else have you seen that you liked?

Decision-making Process

Tell me about the decision-making process at your company.
What is your role in the decision-making process?
Who is involved in the decision-making process?

Time Frame

When would you like the solution to be up and running?
What deadlines should I be aware of?
What will happen between then and now to make that a better time for you?
When will you be ready to place a PO or purchase order?

Budget

How much money do you have set aside for this project?
How are you planning to finance this purchase?
How much money has been approved?
How much would you like to spend?

Decision-making Criteria

What is your preference?
What information do you need to make a decision?
On what factors do you base a decision?
What is the procedure at your company for making a decision like this?

How Do I Win?

What will it take to earn your business and move forward with this solution?
What will it take to choose our product/service?
How do I win?

Next Steps

What happens now?
Where do we go from here?
Who else do you recommend that I speak to?

CLOSING THE CALL

Have you ever hung up from a call and thought to yourself, "Wait a minute, who's doing what?"

Just as in a person-to-person meeting, it's necessary to summarize the conversation before leaving (or hanging up) so that the right hand knows what the left hand is doing. The following closing tips will help you end the call with a clear picture of what must be done.

- **Ask your questions**! Use precise questions to get the information you need.

- **Summarize the answers** to ensure that you and your tele-partner have a mutual understanding.

- **Review the tasks** you and your tele-partner need to do and when they need to be completed. If in a tele-conference, review what each person needs to do.

- **Agree** on when to make the next contact and who will initiate it.

- **End on an upbeat**. Using cliches such as "Have a nice day" tend to be boring and not heartfelt. Use information from your interaction to close. For example, if you and your tele-partner are overdue for a lunch date, say something like, "Julie, it was great speaking with you. Let's set a date for lunch on our next call."

MORE IDEAS FOR CREATING WIN-WIN COMMUNICATIONS

The Upset Customer

Your company receives few questions or complaints, so you believe that customers are satisfied with your products and services. Well, think again. Research done by Technical Assistance Research Program (TARP), Inc. has found that how customer problems and questions are handled determines whether the customer remains loyal. Nothing is more important in business than a loyal customer. Loyal customers are the best form of advertising, so ensuring that every interaction ends positively pays worthwhile dividends. Let's learn to calm those less-than-happy customers and give them the best service possible!

The following ten steps will help you transform that upset telephone customer into a loyal one.

- Smile before answering the telephone. The customer will hear it.

- Identify yourself and ask how you can help.

- Listen! Avoid interrupting the caller and listen well to determine the problem.

- Stay calm. Remember that the customer is not upset with you, so don't take it personally.

- Apologize for the problem and mean it! Customers can tell if they are given lip service.

- Empathize with the customer and use his or her name. Statements such as, "I can appreciate why you are upset, Mr. Touchtone," can go a long way.
- Ask questions to get details.
- Repeat the problem back to the customer using his words.
- Tell the customer what solutions you can offer.
- Repeat your name and offer your phone number. Thank the caller for the opportunity to work with him.

Watch What You Say! The Unintended Statement

Throughout this book, we have talked about creating a 4C Image, and you've seen how that image can turn from negative to positive and vice versa in an instant. Certain phrases that we commonly use tend to give a negative image unintentionally. Let's review a few of these phrases so that you can avoid them in the future.

- *He's disappeared from his desk. Can I have him call you back?* It is better to say, "He's not available at the moment. May I have your name and phone number so that he can return your call?"
- *Mary's still at break/coffee/lunch.* It sounds as if she's late. Watch your use of the word still. Use the same response as above.
- *Ms. Domino went for some blood work. She'll be back in an hour.* Don't share private information with a caller.
- *She left early.* Consider this private information also.
- *They didn't answer again? They always do that! I'll try one more time for you.* Don't air dirty laundry in public. It's none of the caller's business if your com-

pany has an in-house conflict. Keep your statements positive. Instead, say, "I'm sorry you're having trouble connecting. Let me try that number again for you."

Think about phrases you use on a daily basis. As we often say negative things without realizing it, you may be surprised at what you catch yourself saying.

THE POWER OF 800 NUMBERS

Recently a survey on toll-free number usage was initiated by the Society of Consumer Affairs Professionals in Business (SOCAP), conducted by TARP, and sponsored by AT&T. The study found that, depending on the cost of the service or product and the severity of the problem, 20 to 80 percent of the customers who encounter some type of difficulty chose not to contact the company or its distributors. The three reasons for not contacting the company were:

- It was not worth their time.
- It would not have done any good because they felt that no one in the company would do anything about the problem.
- They did not know how or where to contact the company.

This information is especially important in light of TARP findings that negative word of mouth is spread and believed at twice the rate of positive word of mouth. That's a lot of lost business because of negativity on the part of the consumer. Along comes the toll-free number to save the day. TARP studies show that customer service toll-free numbers bridge the gap by providing an easy way for the consumer to contact the company. A highly visible number can double the amount of customer contacts resulting in a more satisfied customer.

The study shows that toll-free numbers provide:

- Increased customer satisfaction and loyalty.
- Increased positive word of mouth.
- Enhanced corporate image.
- Decreased service costs.
- Enhanced product design and quality.
- Decreased customer-caused problems.
- Untapped sources of revenue.

Take all the above advantages, add a little ingenuity, and toll-free numbers can offer any company exciting ways of servicing the customer. Read how Rey Carr, Ph.D. and the folks of Peer Resources, in Victoria, British Columbia, turned what some companies may consider an inconvenience into customer service at its best.

"Our corporation has had a toll-free telephone number for a number of years," says Carr. "When the line was first installed, the staff reported that they got a number of calls that were for wrong numbers. I asked the staff members answering the phone how we might deal with this phenomenon. Here is the approach we came up with and what has happened as a result.

"Rather than just saying, 'you've got the wrong number,' the staff try to find out what number or organization the person is trying to reach. We now keep a file of the various wrong-number organizations (typically they have toll-free numbers that are one digit off from ours), and we provide them with the correct number. It's sort of a directory assistance without the charges.

"We will also call the wrong-number organization and let them know what we are doing and ask them if they would do the same for us, should anyone call them looking for our organization. This request for mutual exchange is not often welcomed at the telephone answer person level, and my staff has reported that more often than not, the person they talk to seems not to care about it . . . Maybe this would have to be discussed at a higher level in their organization in order to develop a service-oriented policy. This practice has led to at least three interesting outcomes, none of which we anticipated when we started this practice:

- "A national association printed our number by mistake in their brochure as the number to call to get information about skiing in Quebec. We immediately tracked down the mistake, called the association to tell them, found out the correct number, and let them know we would redirect the calls to the correct number. The association asked us how many of our employees enjoyed skiing, and then sent us season ski passes for two local ski resorts, which just happen to be the best ski resorts in Canada.

- "On several occasions, callers learning they had connected to the wrong number expressed curiosity about our corporation. Our staff gives them a brief overview and offers to send them some literature about our services. On one occasion, this 'mistake' led to a contract for services.

- "Rather than experiencing the wrong number as an annoying phone call, our staff members typically feel pretty good after such a call, because it provides them an opportunity to be helpful to others. One person even called back (they had to get our number from directory assistance) to tell a staff member that they had experienced a more satisfying interaction with our staff (the wrong number) than they had with the company they were originally trying to reach."

Thanks, Rey, for the outstanding examples. Hopefully, your successes will influence others to set up their own network.

When speaking with people about toll-free numbers, I often hear that they are happy to take advantage of the number if only they could read it on the business card or letterhead. Companies tend to forget that our aging population appreciates being able to read things easily.

Using words in the body of toll-free numbers makes them easy to remember and great for marketing your organization. For example, my company's toll-free number is 1-888-2WinWin. Easy to remember, but a pain to figure out on the keypad. When displaying toll-free numbers on your business card, letterhead, e-mail signature, or any other form of advertising, add the numerical equivalent next to it in parentheses. Use a font that can be read easily. It's a little thing that delivers great service.

THE WORLD OF WIRELESS COMMUNICATIONS

As of July 24, 1998, there were almost 61 million wireless subscribers in the United States, and the number keeps climbing. Experts claim that by 1999 there will be 200 million users worldwide. What's the attraction of these devices? With a wireless phone you can speak to anyone, at anytime, anywhere in the world. They have thoroughly changed the way we live.

Car Safety

In a national poll, 90 percent of the respondents stated that safety and security are the primary reasons they purchased wireless phones, also commonly known as cell phones. According to the Cellular Telecommunications Industry Association, mobile telephones in cars save lives because emergency services, police, and other assistance are at your fingertips. The numbers are impressive. Almost 30 million calls are made annually (83,000 calls per day) to 9-1-1 and other emergency numbers to report breakdowns, accidents, crime, and drunk drivers.

We've all seen those drivers with their cell phone in one hand and a hamburger and fries in the other. Not real healthy in either the diet or driving department. One would think that the use of cell phones while driving would substantially raise the occurrence of accidents, but studies are showing otherwise.

Ten activities that are considered potentially distracting were measured in a survey conducted by *Prevention Magazine*. Cell phone use is not high on the list. Interestingly, 64 percent of those surveyed said they divert their attention from the road when reaching to change a cassette tape or CD while their car is in motion. Of those drivers, only 18 percent reported talking on a mobile phone while driving.

A 1993 study conducted at the University of Michigan Transportation Research Institute found that changing a tape cassette was found to be more distracting than talking on a car phone, and reading a map was almost twice as distracting as talking on a car phone. Noisy children, unrestrained pets, and smoking were all found to be more distracting than using cell phones in a 1995 survey undertaken by Honolulu law enforcement officials.

Does all this mean that it's all right to drive and talk on your phone at the same time? The responsibility ultimately lies with the driver, but there are ways to do it safely. That means buckling up with both hands on the wheel and eyes on the road. The wireless industry suggests that wireless phone users do the following when driving:

- **Use a hands-free phone or speakerphone**. This is the safest way to talk and drive.

- **Use the memory/speed-dialing feature**. It minimizes distractions because you dial the number by pressing one button instead of many. Some phones have voice-activated dialing, which simplifies the process even more. Dialing a phone while driving can be quite a challenge, especially for the baby boomer set, like myself, whose eyes aren't what they used be.

■ **Position your phone where it's easy to see and reach**. Familiarize yourself with the phone before you drive so you're comfortable using it on the road.

■ **When dialing manually, dial only when stopped**. Speed dialing is a great feature, but if you don't have it, pull over to dial or have the passenger dial. If you can't stop or pull over, dial a few digits, then survey traffic before completing the call.

■ **Never take notes while driving**. Note taking and driving don't mix. Pull off the road to a safe spot in order to jot something down.

■ **Use voice mail to pick up calls**. When it's inconvenient or unsafe to answer the car phone, let your wireless network's voice mail pick up your calls. You can even use your voice mail to leave yourself reminders.

■ **Be a wireless Samaritan**. Dialing 9-1-1 is a free call for wireless subscribers. Use it to report crimes in progress or other potentially life-threatening emergencies, accidents, or drunk-driving sightings.

Happy driving!

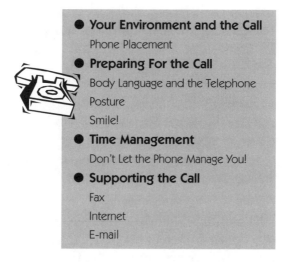

CHAPTER FOUR

Phone Management: Who's Winning ... You or the Phone?

YOUR ENVIRONMENT AND THE CALL

Organize your office before you make or take calls so that in those valuable first seconds you can present the best impression possible. A disorganized office can be heard over the telephone. For example, when you call to leave a message and the person taking the call can't find anything to write with, you can hear him fumbling around, rustling papers and opening drawers, searching for a writing implement. Really impressive, isn't it? Searching for documents in an office piled high with stacks of paper in every corner delivers the same negative impression in addition to decreasing efficiency and appearing unprofessional. An organized environment avoids these scenarios and enables you

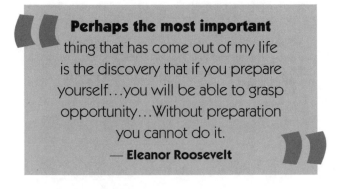

> **Perhaps the most important**
> thing that has come out of my life
> is the discovery that if you prepare
> yourself...you will be able to grasp
> opportunity...Without preparation
> you cannot do it.
> — **Eleanor Roosevelt**

to serve the customer quickly and efficiently. A properly organized work environment also helps to ensure that you and your company are presenting a 4C Image.

Phone Placement

Preparing your desk—whether it's in an office, cubicle, or on the kitchen table—takes thought and planning. If you are setting up your office from scratch, note where the electrical outlets and telephone jacks are located in the room. I have seen people set up their entire office and have everything exactly as they want it, only to realize that the electrical outlets and phone jack are on the other side of the room. Thank goodness for extension cords!

Before you hook up your telephone, sit at your desk and relax in your chair. Close your eyes, and in your mind's eye see yourself answering the phone. Ask yourself these questions:

■ Do you have difficulty reaching the telephone?

■ Do you knock anything over with your hand or arm when reaching for the phone?

■ Does the receiver or cord hit anything when you pick it up?

■ Do you need to hunt for pen and paper to take a message?

■ Do you switch the receiver from one hand to the other so that you can write?

■ Do you cradle the phone between your neck and shoulder?

If you answer "yes" to any of these questions, then the telephone may not be properly positioned on your desk. Placing it in the right spot will increase job performance by saving time and allowing you to answer the call in a fluid and professional manner. Let's examine each question.

Do you have difficulty reaching the telephone? Most people place the phone on the desk to mirror their dominant hand. It should be no farther away than an arm's length. Anything farther than that is inefficient.

Do you knock anything over with your hand or arm when reaching for the phone? If you usually have a drink sitting in the line of fire of the telephone, have a mop, bucket, or a roll of paper towels close by. Avoid placing a beverage, picture frame, flower vase, or anything else that your hand or arm can knock over close to or in front of your phone.

Does the receiver or cord hit anything when you pick it up? If possible, make sure there are no obstructions to the receiver's flight path from the cradle to your ear. In this case, I'm talking specifically about things such as low-hanging desk hutches or shelving. I speak with the voice of experience on this one. The design of my desk hutch forces me to place my phone in only one place. Directly above it are cabinets. More than once, especially when moving quickly, I have banged the receiver on the bottom of the cabinets when answering a call. I found that I was able to alleviate the problem by adjusting the height of my chair.

Do you need to hunt for pen and paper to take a message? Keep items such as blank purchase orders, price lists, product information, or any other materials that you use for your job within close reach. Have writing materials by the telephone, and stash a supply in a hidden place in your desk if you have "borrowers." Keep a notebook, pen, and good-quality sticky message pad, either blank or preprinted, by the phone. When using the notebook to record your calls and take notes, it's helpful to write the date at the top of the page as a point of reference for reviewing your notes later. When taking messages for coworkers, place sticky notes right on their telephones, computer monitors, or keyboards. Some people say to put the note on the back or seat of their chairs. Frankly, I would sit on it.

Sticky pads are wonderful inventions. Good-quality pads are best because they stick better to a surface and thus reduce the risk of losing the note. I have bought inexpensive brands and found that they're no better than working with plain scratch paper. They just don't stick well. Use the sticky pads to write down your information, then tear off the sheet and place it in an obvious place. I place my notes on the cabinet door of my hutch so that they are always in my line of vision. When I'm finished with the note, I toss it out.

Do you switch the receiver from one hand to the other so that you can write? If your desk arrangement allows, place the phone on the side of your nondominant hand and answer it with that hand. The advantage is that you have the freedom of writing without switching hands. It may take some practice to get used to this new arrangement, but it places you in perfect position to write the moment you pick up the receiver.

Do you cradle the phone between your neck and shoulder? This is a classic. The phone rings and you pick it up with your dominant hand. To take a message or write notes, you immediately do the "pain in the neck shuffle" by placing the receiver between your ear and shoulder. If the method in the previous question doesn't work for you and you must continue to do the "pain in the neck shuffle," purchase a shoulder rest. It's not foolproof, but it does help. Shoulder rests tend to place your chin on the mouthpiece making it difficult to speak distinctly and clearly, so be careful.

If you are a heavy phone user, a headset is the best way to ensure free hands and cramp-free neck and shoulders. Plantronics, the leading manufacturer of headsets, commissioned H.B. Maynard and Company to perform a research study on headset use. The participants of the study included salespeople, travel agents, technical field sales support people, and stockbrokers who were familiar with headset use. The results were astounding. The workers using headsets were 43 percent more productive. Repeat calls were made without interruption, and time-intensive tasks (such as typing or checking reference materials while on the phone) were performed far more quickly and efficiently.

Another part of the study that was equally impressive was that workers equipped with headsets reported higher morale, lower fatigue levels, and fewer phone-related physical complaints. They also commented that after more than a week with headsets, returning to bulky, cumbersome, handheld phones was "inconceivable." A good source for all brands of headsets is Hello Direct (1-800-444-3556).

PREPARING FOR THE CALL

The telephone was designed to allow human interaction between two people at two different locations to take place over a wire. The system is useless unless a person, fax, or modem picks up the receiver at the other end of the call. Let's focus on what happens when two people connect with each other using the telephone. Remember, the telephone is only as effective as the person who operates it. Use it well and the benefits are tremendous.

Body Language and the Telephone

Can you hear body language over the telephone? Absolutely! If you really listen, you can "see" someone slouched over his desk just from the tone of voice. Now picture that person sitting straight and tall, and you will get a completely different image of the individual speaking to you over the telephone. Research shows that good posture projects health, vitality, and confidence, while hunching suggests weakness, gloom, and self-doubt. By changing your posture, you can change how you are perceived when you make a call.

Posture

Studies show that up to 20 percent of the people in the United States and 50 percent of the working population suffer from some sort of back and/or neck pain every year. Poor posture can cause ailments such as lower-back pain, chronic neck pain, and headache. Slumping over your desk leaves less room for your lungs to fill with oxygen and may even cause decreased lung capacity. This, in turn, adversely affects how you breathe, thereby depleting your body's available energy.

Good posture requires maintaining the natural S curve of the spine. The ear, shoulder, hip, and knee should be in alignment. When sitting, standing, or walking, imagine a cord attached to the crown of your head pulling you up to the heavens. Then imagine that same cord passing through

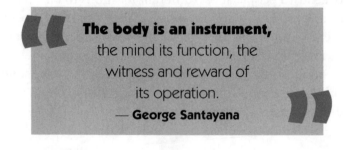

The body is an instrument, the mind its function, the witness and reward of its operation.
— **George Santayana**

your body and exiting your feet into the earth. This alignment opens up the body and allows it the ability to breathe well and energize.

Posture can also affect attitude. Unhappy or depressed people may dip their heads and shoulders forward. Stretching and breathing deeply for two minutes at various times throughout the day helps to alleviate tension and improve attitude. If you are stressed or unhappy, callers can hear it in your voice.

Your office chair should be comfortable and fit your body well. If you sit at your desk for long periods of time, a footrest will reduce strain on your lower back, legs, and feet. If you work at a computer, place your monitor at eye level.

As a teenager, my friends and I made up a telephone game that we loosely called "Guess My Position." We would lie on our backs or stomachs, stand, sit, slouch, put our elbows on the table, or prop our heads in our hands. We would then attempt to guess what position the other person was in, and we were usually right! Without seeing each other, we could decipher the other's position based on breathing patterns, voice tones, speech, and voice volume.

This teenage game illustrates the importance of good posture when communicating over the telephone. If you tune in to the person calling you and listen carefully, you may be surprised at what you hear and the mental images that you "see."

Smile!

Whenever we became bored, my teenaged friends and I varied the "Guess My Position" game by making faces at a handheld mirror and talking into the phone. It then became the "Guess What I'm Feeling" game. We could tell what the other person was feeling by guessing what face she was making. We were able to detect an angry, happy, sad, frustrated, or shocked face based on the other person's speech and tone of voice. Little did we know how much we were learning as we were playing.

Of all of the faces we loved to make in our mirrors, we most enjoyed the laughing face and the smiling face. The laughing face brought us to our knees. We really felt good afterwards. It was so contagious that even our parents laughed as they monitored our telephone time. The smiling face is still the most important of all our faces. My friends and I made a pact that we would neither answer nor hang up the phone until we had smiles on our faces. At an early age, we learned the power of a smile.

Telemarketers have known the usefulness of keeping a mirror by their desks to remind them to smile. I highly recommend doing this when answering or making a call. It really does work.

TIME MANAGEMENT

Planning your day is part of being successful. You make a game plan and execute it to reach your goals. Sounds simple, right? All of a sudden, the day ends and your game plan is out the window because you could not get away from the telephone. If this keeps happening to you, it's time to take action.

Don't Let the Phone Manage You!

If the telephone is a major part of your job, then it's important to plan your day around it. Since time is money in business, the following tips will help you save precious minutes:

- Use the phone placement techniques offered in the beginning of this chapter to help save time.

- Use an answering machine to take calls. Tell the customer the exact information you want him or her to leave. *Hello, you have reached Bangers and Mash Associates. At the sound of the tone, please leave your name, telephone number, and your message, and we will return your call shortly. Thanks for calling.*

▪ Block a specific time each day to answer your machine messages and return calls. Return all calls within twenty-four hours (forty-eight hours maximum). It's best to return them the same day.

▪ When you are put on hold for long periods of time, do simple things that you normally put off. For example, enter information from business cards or notes into your database. Stop when your party comes back on the line.

▪ Another tip for when you are on hold for long periods is to put the call on speakerphone. If your telephone has that feature, you can continue working until your party comes back to the phone. Then pick up the receiver to continue the call.

▪ If the person you must call is a "talker," leave a message during off-hours when he is not around, or send him an e-mail or fax.

SUPPORTING THE CALL

Everyone wants information immediately, and our state-of-the-art technology provides businesses and consumers with various ways to get it. Employees require solid training in the use of facsimile machines, computers, e-mail, the Internet, and the telephone because consumers are quite savvy in the use of these tools. Sales departments, marketing departments, and call centers must be prepared to receive and deliver information in whatever method the customer chooses. Regardless of the medium used when communicating with the consumer, the first impression must be a 4C Image. If a customer calls on the telephone and requests that information be faxed or e-mailed, you should be able to respond accordingly.

Fax

It is nearly impossible to conduct business without a fax machine and a computer fax/modem. A fax machine makes easy work of sending invoices, letters, proposals, price lists, and any other written or printed document. Any kind of document, from technical information to your kids' drawings for their grandparents, can be faxed in an instant. Exceptions that should be sent by conventional mail (or snail mail) are invitations that are written, typed, or engraved on good paper stock. Sympathy cards, thank-you notes, a congratulatory letter, or other important documents should also be sent via conventional mail. Imagine going to a black-tie event carrying a fax as your invitation!

Just as a letter is sent in an envelope, a fax should be sent with a cover sheet so that it is delivered to the correct person. Your name and your company's name, address, and phone number should appear on the cover sheet. The phone number makes it easy for the person to contact you if a response is required. Avoid sending anything personal by fax. You never know who will pick it up and read it in an office that shares fax machines.

Avoid being what etiquette expert Leticia Baldridge calls "fax-rude." Just as unsolicited junk mail can be annoying, so can unsolicited junk faxes. This practice ties up the telephone lines and uses the recipient's expensive paper. If a need to send a long fax arises, call the recipient beforehand and inform her that the fax is being sent. She may wish to have it mailed instead.

Computers with a fax/modem can hold faxes without printing them. This saves paper, although the fax line can be tied up if it's a long document. The beauty of a fax/modem is that the message can be viewed on the computer monitor. The computer operator may then choose to either print or delete the message.

Increasing numbers of entrepreneurs are setting up home offices, and there is a growing trend among companies that allows employees to telecommute from home. For these reasons, fax machines are now quite common in private residences. Furthermore, technological advancements afford us the opportunity to do business twenty-four hours a day with virtually anyone in the world. However, be aware of the time that you send faxes. Receiving a fax at 3 a.m., especially an unsolicited one, does not endear one to the sender when it wakes up the family.

A fax-on-demand system saves valuable time by allowing customers to access frequently requested information. It is also quick and efficient. After dialing into the system, this service permits clients to choose from a menu that contains previously stored faxes. An automatic attendant guides the caller through the menu and helps the caller choose the information he wants. The automatic attendant asks for the caller's fax number and, within minutes, the client receives the information.

Internet

Today, the most visible way to market products and services worldwide is through the Internet. It has changed how the world does business, and it's here to stay. A Web site makes as powerful a first impression as a brochure, ad materials, or a personal meeting.

According to the American Internet User Survey, more than 41.5 million U.S. adults were actively using the Internet in 1997. The study claims that this is an increase of 33 percent over the second quarter of 1997. "The number of adults on-line continued to grow dramatically in the second half of the year, confirming a growing dependency on the Internet," says Thomas E. Miller, vice president of Cyber Dialogue and developer of the American Internet User Survey.

The survey also found that 23.8 million adults expressed interest in signing up for Internet access within the next twelve months, an increase of more than two million from the second quarter of 1997. "Internet usage will continue to grow for the next five years," Miller says, "but the market will become much more segmented as the medium becomes more mainstream and user preferences become more divergent."

The survey provided the following points:

- 58% of current adult Internet users are male; 42% are female.

- 51% of Web users use the Internet on a daily basis.

- 87% of Internet users agree with the statement: "The Internet provides more efficient access to information I need every day."

- 77% of adults who use the Internet predominantly for work agree that: "On-line services have made me more productive at my job."

A Web site is vital to a company's marketing tool kit. It allows the customer to find you easily. You can refer customers with Internet access to the company Web site for information that they request. It's fast, convenient, and economical. It reduces printing and mailing fees, and the customer doesn't wait for the information. It's at his fingertips any time of day or night.

Affordable software can put any business on the Internet. A business Web site should include the same information that is in a brochure, but much more, because you are telling the world who you are. Information such as product descriptions, price lists, articles, press releases, company history, and frequently asked questions and answers about products and services are ideal for this medium. The choices are endless.

A good Web site includes several ways for the customer to contact you. List the company's telephone number, fax number, and an e-mail address. If the customer contacts you via e-mail, ask him or her to provide the following information:

- A short message describing the customer's request.

- The customer's return e-mail address.

- How the customer wants the information delivered (e-mail, fax, or telephone).

- If the customer wants a return phone call, and the best time to call.

E-mail

Just like the Internet, e-mail is here to stay. It's quick, easy, and inexpensive, and it's the most casual way to communicate globally. Unfortunately, the casual mentality has caused people to believe that spelling, punctuation, and grammar are not important. Nothing could be further from the truth.

Every six weeks for the last eight years, I've delivered a Career Image program to military personnel who are either retiring or separating from the service. E-mail is always a colorful topic during class. Once, from the back of the room, a booming voice proclaimed: "I was told that spelling and grammar aren't important when writing e-mail because it's a quick and fast way to communicate." I quickly set the gentleman straight. Not caring about the presentation and detail of any written communication is unprofessional and gives a you-are-not-important message to the recipient. This man, a well-educated Navy captain and accomplished leader, was seeking a management position in the civilian world. What image will he project to his new customers and employer if he believes that mistakes are acceptable?

Misspelling, poor punctuation, and poor grammar might affect your relationship with your customer in the following ways:

Customer e-mail message to you: *Dear Ms. Waterpitcher: I just visited your Web site and really enjoyed it. I'm interested in receiving more information about your customer service course. Please contact me as soon as possible. Regards, Susie Cottonswab.*

Your reply: *Tahkyou for contacint Waterpitcher Associates. We atke pride in serving our cusotmers. You will like our catalog but before wi can send it yuo we need yor addresss Thanks for contacting us we look forward to seving yo. Teeery Waterpichetr.*

Do you think that Susie Cottonswab would want to hire me based on the above response? I don't think so. Why should she send someone to our courses based on the shoddiness of the message? The message has an I-don't-care attitude and does not demonstrate the 4Cs: Confidence, Competence, Credibility, and Congruence. When it comes to your professional image, never let your guard down, and that includes writing e-mail messages.

A few rules govern this type of correspondence:

- Use both upper and lower case letters in your messages. IF YOU USE ONLY CAPITAL LETTERS, YOUR READERS WILL THINK THAT YOU ARE YELLING AT THEM!

- It's acceptable to take three days to respond to e-mail, but I recommend the same twenty-four hour time frame suggested for the telephone.

- Use a salutation and closing.

- Include your name, position, company name, phone number, fax number, and e-mail address in your "signature." Virtually all e-mail programs will automatically append programmed information to the end of every message sent out.

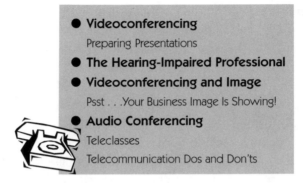

CHAPTER FIVE

Teleconferencing

Imagine being a nine-year-old visitor to the 1964 World's Fair. You feel the excitement of that wonderland as you race from exhibit to exhibit. The AT&T pavilion beckons you to leave your world behind and enter into the future. People around you are talking into funny-looking telephones. Others are chattering at TV screens while holding boxes with buttons that they press as they speak. You wait in line to try this machine for what seems like an eternity to your impatient nine years. Your turn finally arrives, and you realize that the person speaking to you on the screen is coming to you from Disneyland! Geez, are you on the wrong end of that call!

The equipment displayed at the World's Fair that day was an experimental system called a Picturephone. Slow and bulky, the device transmitted a new image every two seconds. The public was not quite enamored with this less-than-user-friendly device. In 1970, in Pittsburgh, Pennsylvania, AT&T debuted a commercial version of the Picturephone with the hope that one million of the devices would be in use by 1980. Wrong number.

The 1990s became the decade when AT&T's vision of personal video communications would come to fruition. In 1993, the Picturephone's descendant, the Model 70, was incorporated into the computer, a piece of equipment that has transformed the way we live. Communicating in the workplace now includes a colleague's video visage on your computer screen as you simultaneously collaborate, annotate, and edit files with the click of a mouse or the press of a key on your keyboard. Videoconferencing at its best!

VIDEOCONFERENCING

Quickly becoming a workplace staple, you can find videoconferencing in corporate America, in schools, at medical facilities, and in corner copy centers. You can hold any size meeting or conference at any time via a computer monitor, television, or big screen—thus saving valuable time and travel expenses. Whether large or small, in Alaska or Maine, groups can now communicate with each other with ease. You can use videoconferencing for:

- workshops and seminars
- speeches
- distance learning
- business and management meetings
- training sessions
- brainstorming sessions
- management and staff development
- project collaboration
- sales presentations

Software such as Microsoft Powerpoint or Corel Presentations can make already powerful presentations even more so. Slides and video appear on the screen, allowing everyone who participates in the videoconference to collaborate and deliver feedback.

Videoconferencing does have its drawbacks, however. Common meeting tools such as flip charts and white boards are ineffective in this medium. Flip charts are cumbersome and can be difficult to read. Every noise made when flipping the charts over or tearing off sheets of paper is amplified by microphones. Not a great image. Standard white boards create a glare that makes reading the information on them difficult even under the best lighting. In this medium, testing the lighting beforehand is imperative.

Today's technology provides the solutions to these dilemmas with software such as GroupBoard by PictureTel. The software, which simulates standard meeting tools such as flip charts and white boards, allows participants the freedom and flexibility to deliver presentations, brainstorm, sketch ideas, mark up visuals, and print the results at multiple sites.

Preparing Presentations

Preparing and delivering presentations takes a lot of time and hard work. Follow these videoconferencing tips to ensure a 4C Image:

- Avoid rooms with noisy air conditioning or ventilation. It's distracting to everyone!
- Use a room with appropriate lighting. Today's cameras do not require as much light as in the past.
- Don't point a camera at a window.
- The presenter should avoid standing in front of a window. All that will be seen is his silhouette.

- Ensure that furniture or decorative accessories do not block anyone's vision.

- Have the correct number of cameras for the size of the group. The following numbers are ideal (your budget will dictate how much equipment you can afford): For three to five people, have two cameras; for five and above, have three to four cameras. Placing a camera at each wall allows the use of wide-angle shots.

- Avoid tapping fingers or pens on the table surface. The microphones will pick up these sounds, and they are as aggravating in a videoconference as they are in person.

- Avoid shuffling papers. The microphone picks up everything!

- No Khrushchev-style fist pounding on the table.

- Beware of open table microphones.

Microphones are an essential part of videoconferencing, so it's necessary to learn how to use them well. Watch your words when you are using microphones because being caught unaware by an open mike can be most embarrassing. Tony Alessandra, author of the Platinum Rule and a seasoned videoconference presenter, offers these three tips when presenting or attending a multiple site videoconference.

- If you are the presenter and you are wearing a portable mike, make sure it's turned off when you are off stage…especially before entering the bathroom.

- If you are a participant in a satellite videoconference, and there are both cameras and microphones at your location, watch your words and actions when entering the room before the program. The presenter, regardless of which satellite location she is in, may be able to hear and see, which could be most embarrassing for you.

■ Remember that the camera can focus on you at any time, so watch your posture and avoid picking your teeth. You don't want the presenter in California seeing every tooth and filling!

Videoconferencing to multiple sites can also be successful using one-way video and audio. In these programs, the speaker presents to an in-house audience. The presentation is viewed in real time at satellite locations where questions can be asked via fax. The presenter reads the faxed questions and answers into the camera. The advantage here is lower cost without an appreciable loss of effectiveness.

THE HEARING-IMPAIRED PROFESSIONAL

How difficult is it for a deaf professional in a hearing world to communicate? While doing research on the Internet, I logged on to several Web sites dealing with deafness. I wanted to phone these organizations, but no phone numbers were given. Then it dawned on me that there were no phone numbers because a hearing-impaired person is unable to communicate with me without special equipment.

Communicating over the telephone is not possible for the deaf person without using a special device called a Telecommunications Device for the Deaf (TDD), also known as a teletypewriter (TTY). When the phone rings, the deaf person places the receiver on a coupler attached to the TTY device. The device has a small keyboard and the communication takes place by typing back and forth. Naturally, a TDD must be available at both ends of the call for communication to take place. Relay services are available that mediate communication between TDD and voice calls. The relay-service operator types what the hearing person says, then reads aloud what the deaf person types. Relay services, which are provided by telephone companies, are usually listed in the front of the phone book.

More than four million people in the United States with hearing or severe speech impairments communicate with finger spelling and sign language, lip reading, pen and paper, fax machines, and e-mail as well as TDD.

In the past, videoconferencing was an ineffective method of communicating for the deaf professional due to slow video frame speeds. Individuals fluent in sign language found it especially difficult. In February 1998, a company called 8x8, Inc. introduced new equipment that provides video communications specifically for hearing-impaired individuals. This new technology marries video and text communications over a standard telephone line. The product, VideoTTY Videophones, allows users to enjoy simultaneous video and text communications over a plain old telephone service (POTS) line by using an infrared keyboard and an on-screen text display. It works with televisions, video cameras, or camcorders, and any standard TTY unit. No computer expense!

One model includes Internet access and send/receive e-mail capability. Quite an accomplishment. The video allows for use of sign language to augment the text and offers an additional means for deaf professionals to communicate with their clients and coworkers.

Other companies produce videophone equipment for deaf people. BigPicture TV phone, sold by 3Com, is based on 8x8's technology. C-Phone Corp. in North Carolina sells a higher quality videophone that costs about $1,000 and requires a digital ISDN. Additionally, Fremont-based Advis produces a videophone called the AD-20, which promises higher performance for customers with two phone lines.

The key to successful communication with a deaf person is to help him or her see what is being said as clearly as possible. Videoconferencing may soon become a part of every deaf professional's tool kit.

When including a deaf or hard-of-hearing person in a video teleconference, the following meeting tips from the Betty and Leonard Phillips Deaf Action Center of Louisiana help ensure that everyone connects, regardless of the method used to communicate.

- Participants should be seated so that all individuals are within "eye reach."
- The deaf person should sit at the end of a rectangular table.
- Speakers should give a visual signal before starting to speak. It is perfectly acceptable to tap a person lightly on the shoulder or arm, wave a hand or small piece of paper gently in the person's direction, or give some other visual signal to attract his or her attention.
- Only one person at a time should speak.
- Deaf participants should sit next to the note taker. The note taker should enter the name or initials of each speaker next to his or her comments so that the deaf person can review the notes after the meeting.
- Face the deaf person and maintain eye contact throughout the conversation.
- Stand close to the deaf person when speaking.
- Make sure the person sees your entire face. Don't eat, smoke, chew gum, or hold your hands in front of your mouth, because many deaf people read lips. Take off dark glasses so that your eyes are visible.
- Don't talk while you are writing. When writing, you look down, and the deaf person is unable to see your face and mouth clearly.
- Speak and enunciate clearly and normally without exaggerating or emphasizing your lip movements. Use

your voice, but don't shout. Many deaf people can get some information through sound, but shouting distorts both the sound of words and the lip movements.

■ Use large, broad facial expressions and body language to clarify your message. Don't assume that a bland expression implies a deaf person is catching what you say.

■ Don't assume that a deaf person will be able to lip-read long or unusual words.

■ Rephrase sentences that deaf clients don't understand. Don't repeat the same words over and over in the same sequence.

■ Speak directly to the deaf person, not to the interpreter.

■ Don't be embarrassed to write things down. Write technical or difficult vocabulary on the board the first time it is presented. Use pencil and paper or visual aids as necessary.

VIDEOCONFERENCING AND IMAGE

The image you project in a videoconference is just as important as the image you project when meeting someone in person. Because first impressions based solely on physical appearance are made within seconds, the attention you pay to your wardrobe and overall presence is time well invested.

Advertisers and manufacturers spend millions of dollars annually in the physical marketing of their products. Color, design, and texture are all critical to successful product packaging. On the screen, you are the product. How you package and present yourself is an important factor when communicating with others. To be successful, present yourself in the most effective and polished manner possible. In other words, present yourself with the 4C Image of Confidence, Competence, Credibility, and Congruence.

Let's do a quick exercise. Imagine meeting someone for the first time as she is about to enter your office. In slow motion, watch the door open and envision the person entering the room. Notice the following facial expressions and body movements:

- Is she smiling, frowning, or tense?
- Does the person deliver a strong or weak handshake?
- Is she looking you in the eyes or staring at the floor?
- Is she wearing her clothes or are they wearing her?
- Is her tone of voice soft, weak, loud, in control?
- Does she speak quickly or slowly?
- Does she appear in control and confident, or does she lack confidence?
- Overall, is she slow-paced or fast-paced?
- Is she mannerly (e.g., sits when asked to and not before)?

Now run this same scene in your mind's eye at a normal pace. How long does it take for you to create an impression of this person? It certainly doesn't take long to paint the picture in your mind, does it? When you meet someone in person, you form a first impression within four seconds. Within four minutes the impression, positive or negative, may become permanent.

When I present my *Psst…Your Business Image Is Showing* program, I have the participants view slides of men and women before and after a makeover. They are asked to state what kind of job the person in the slide holds. Unknown to the class is that their emotional responses to the slides are being timed by two of the participants. Everything from "Wow" to "Is that the same person?" is often heard. At the end of the fifteen-minute exercise, I ask the timers to calculate the average response time to the slides. Based solely on individual appearance, it only takes 1.5 to 3.5 seconds to form an impression. Some people are in awe of how fast first impressions are created, and others get upset. The latter don't believe that they form first impressions solely on appearance. Yet we all cross the street or move to the other side of the pavement to avoid a person that we perceive as strange. It may be terrible that we behave this way, but, as human beings, we are programmed by nature to react in certain ways to those things which appeal to us or repel us visually.

The cost of computer video is now within reach of the average person, and videoconferencing is rapidly becoming a standard mode of communication for both corporate America and home offices. Those of us who work at home have been spoiled by being able to dress as we please, without worry of looking professional. Our professional voice has tended to carry the day. Videophones will certainly alter that comfort zone. Depending on the client, we now need to dress as though attending a business meeting or making a sales call.

Psst...Your Business Image Is Showing!

Imagine that you have a video teleconference scheduled in a few moments. You look around and realize that your videophone "sees" quite a bit of your office—in disaster mode! You look professional, but your surroundings leave a lot to be desired. Is the disaster in view of your caller? That depends on your system. Will it detract from your professionalism? Of course, it will. So, is a videophone a good thing? It depends. Videophones can make any company appear large or small according to the image you present. Your surroundings send major nonverbal signals to your callers.

Let's focus on your appearance during a videoconference. You may be thinking, "Is physical appearance really that important in a videoconference?" Absolutely. If it's important in "real life," then it's important in the videoconference.

Earlier in this chapter, you were told to envision a person entering your office and ask yourself if the clothes were wearing her or was she wearing the clothes? You probably thought that was a silly question, but have you ever met someone who looked as if he were playing "grown-up" because of the way his clothes fit? Start to focus on those around you and note their apparel. Chances are, those who wear their clothes well present a powerful image. Note also that it's the entire package of dress, body language, and confidence that makes a person attractive.

The colors that you wear during a videoconference or on a videophone will send specific messages to the people you are interacting with. Red is a powerful color that gets the adrenaline moving. Blue gives a feeling of competence and confidence that makes you believable. Pink is a feminine color and should be avoided unless worn with a navy or gray suit.

Focus on your television screen the next time you watch the news. Determine which newscasters look good and which ones could use improvement. The following tips will help you to make your best presentation in a videoconference or a television appearance:

■ Avoid wearing clothing with tight patterns. A pinstriped suit designed with the lines close together or a hound's-tooth check fall into this category. These patterns make focusing the camera difficult and give the appearance the garment is moving. Johnny Carson once wore a jacket that created so much movement that he was told to remove it. Johnny's face quickly came back into focus.

- Avoid wild ties. They will be distracting.

- Avoid wearing pure white and black.

- Avoid red, which tends to "ring." Red garments look like they have auras. Have you ever noticed that the edges of a red jacket become fuzzy on television? A woman who wears red lipstick on camera runs the risk of having her mouth appear as if it's moving even when she's not talking. Her message gets lost because viewers focus on her mouth.

- Avoid reflective or noisy jewelry. Microphones easily pick up the noise of bracelets banging on the desk.

- Use an anti-reflective coating on your glasses. If you wear eyeglasses and are frequently before a camera or audience, in sales, or dealing with people daily (which most of us do), have your glasses coated with an anti-reflective product. This coating eliminates the annoying communication barrier that occurs when your eyes can't be seen due to reflection. When I speak on this topic before an audience, I switch my glasses from an anti-reflective pair to a reflective pair to show the difference. Some coatings tend to scratch and peel, which is why I recommend Reflection Free. It's expensive, but well worth the price.

- If it's long enough, sit on the tail of your jacket to pull it down in the back. That way the collar doesn't rise or gap, and you present a much neater appearance.

AUDIO CONFERENCING

Audio conferencing is the easiest and most common way of communicating with several people at the same time by using the telephone. It's perfect for long-distance meetings and distance learning. Larger businesses often have teleconferencing features built right into their phone systems.

What do you do if you are a small business and need to speak with two others who are several hundred miles apart? No problem. Call your local telephone company, sign up for three-way calling, and you've got it. Teleconferencing at its best. Want to speak with two others, but you don't have three-way calling in your area? The problem is easy to solve, though more costly. Add a second phone line, purchase a phone with a conferencing feature, and have each person call you. Press the conference button and again you have the miracle of teleconferencing. Have a speakerphone? Call your party and she can speak to anyone present in the room with you.

Teleclasses

Teleclasses are becoming a means of continuing education for many professionals with busy schedules. According to Leslie Speidel, marketing coach and owner of Small Business University, business leaders everywhere are finding that distance education allows their people to study on their own time and gain new skills that otherwise would not be available. Business expenditures for nontraditional education now far outdistance what is spent on regular university courses.

In these real-time interactive conferences, the participants call a teleconference bridge at a given hour. Depending on the type of equipment used, these bridges accept anywhere from thirty to 150 callers per line. These fully automated systems connect every call immediately. Unless a toll-free number is provided, long-distance charges apply on these calls if you do not live in the calling area where the teleconference bridge is located.

Participating in a class with thirty to 150 other people from different parts of the world is quite an experience. You may think that lack of visual aids and not being able to see your classmates would cause problems, but according to Speidel, the reverse is true. "This medium has great advantages because it does not allow you to form judgments and attitudes based on a participant's physical appearance," she says. "Everyone is equal. Accents may pose a problem, but by listening extra hard and not being afraid to ask someone to repeat a question or statement, barriers come down."

Telecommunication Dos and Don'ts

The following tips on teleconferencing etiquette will guide you to a successful call and help you avoid embarrassment.

■ Call the teleconference bridge number assigned to you at the appointed time. The facilitator is responsible to call, fax, or e-mail the number and agenda to you before the call. Keep the number in a safe place. I write the number along with the time, type of call, and any other pertinent information on my calendar, so that all information is in one place.

■ Once connected, the facilitator or host will welcome you. If you are on a large call, you will be asked for your name and where you are from. Say, for example, "Hi, this is Sally from Iowa." It's important to state where you are from because you could have multiple Sallys on the line. When the facilitator asks for questions and comments, identify yourself the same way. This may not be necessary on a call with only a few people.

- Make sure your environment is as quiet as possible. If you are participating in a teleclass or business teleconference from home, use your mute button where noise cannot be controlled. Dogs barking, children screaming, and television sets or radios blaring in the background are distracting, not only to yourself, but also to other callers on the line.

- If you use a phone with multiple lines, disable the ringers on the other lines to avoid incoming calls from distracting others on the teleconference call. Some multiple-line speakerphones do not have that capability. Mine does not, so I keep my mute button on except to question or make a comment.

- Headsets are wonderful inventions. They take pressure off your neck and shoulders and, by keeping your body in alignment, help save on chiropractor bills. They completely free up your hands so you can take notes efficiently. To be heard and understood clearly while using a headset, place the microphone squarely in front of your mouth. Refer to Chapter 4 for more information on headsets.

- Avoid eating, typing, filing, opening your mail, or rustling papers while on a call. It's distracting and rude.

- Have you ever heard a heavy breather on the phone? The imagination takes over when you experience it, and many people don't realize they are doing it. Pulling the receiver away from your mouth is a quick fix.

- On "large" calls, ask the facilitator for permission to speak if you would like to comment on what someone said or speak to another person on the call. This helps to keep the call in control. For example, if the facilitator's name is Alex, say, "Alex, this is Sally from Iowa. May I ask Michael to repeat what he said about making sushi?"

■ Be respectful of others' viewpoints, even if you disagree. Leslie Speidel tells a story about a class she was facilitating during which two female participants got into a disagreement that sounded more like a brawl: "In the middle of my class, two women started bickering about trademarks and patents. One of the women was a lawyer and considered herself knowledgeable about the topic. The argument escalated until it got out of control. I tried to stop them by saying, 'Ladies,' several times, but it didn't help. Then I said their names, but that didn't work either. Finally, I screamed at them to put on their mute button or get off the call. I said that it was not their call, it was mine. Both women stopped, stunned at their behavior, and hung up. Needless to say, anytime they try to sign up for one of my courses, I tell them the class is full." Imagine if this had happened on a sales call. I don't believe that sale would have been made.

■ Who hasn't experienced the embarrassment of walking late into a meeting? As you melt into your seat, you hope no one notices. When you're late on a large conference call, no one sees you, but if it's a small class, there may be no escaping. Joining any type of teleconference call late is disruptive because your line ringing into the call can be distracting to others already on the line. If you're late, just dial the number and listen quietly until you are up to speed on the discussion. It's better to join a teleconference late than not to participate at all.

■ Don't tape a conference without everyone's permission. It is illegal in the United States to do so.

- If your phone is a speakerphone, don't use it to partici-pate in a teleclass. Speakerphones don't work well on these types of calls; they make it difficult to hear you clearly. Technology is improving them, but for now the handset or a headset is best on these types of calls. The speakerphone is fine for listening in on the class as long as you use your mute button.

- If you use a speakerphone on a business teleconfer-ence, *always* inform the caller that she is on a speaker-phone and introduce her to anyone else that is physi-cally in the room with you. The following story by my good friend, Jan Schwarzenberg, eloquently illustrates the reason for this.

Sally called a favorite cousin at his office one day. When he got on the phone, he asked what she was doing. She replied that she was nursing the baby. After a pregnant pause, her cousin stammered that he wished she wouldn't tell him things like that, which was followed by laughter in the background. Sally asked him where he was. "I'm in a meeting in the conference room, and you're on a speakerphone," her cousin responded.

CHAPTER SIX

Working From Home

THE HOME-BASED OFFICE

Not since the industrial revolution has the American workforce experienced such change. With the rise of the SOHO (Small Office/Home Office), the workplace landscape is shifting dramatically. It used to be that working from home was considered unprofessional. Anyone who had a business in his home was not taken seriously. Indeed, as the 20th century draws to a close, those of us working out of our homes still suffer an overall lack of respect for the sanctity of our residential workstations. Friends pop in unannounced; children's pals race through home offices innocently, yet intrusively; telemarketers tie up home-business phones; utility people make unscheduled visits; neighbors

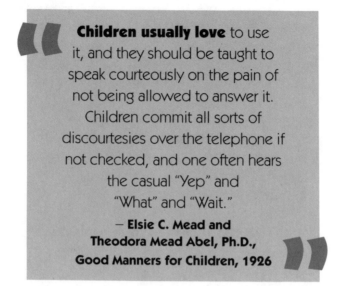

> **Children usually love** to use it, and they should be taught to speak courteously on the pain of not being allowed to answer it. Children commit all sorts of discourtesies over the telephone if not checked, and one often hears the casual "Yep" and "What" and "Wait."
>
> — **Elsie C. Mead and Theodora Mead Abel, Ph.D., Good Manners for Children, 1926**

allow dogs to bark incessantly. We are, however, making headway.

A trick that some business owners once used to appear larger and more professional was to have a cassette tape of office sounds, such as typewriters, playing in the background. It worked! Well, welcome to the 1990s and the dawn of the new millennium. Working from home has a new image, and millions are doing it with style.

Telecommuting

Eureka! Gail's boss just approved her request to telecommute from home. What an opportunity! After two years of talking and negotiating, her boss reluctantly agreed to a six-month trial. Working from home will make life so easy. No more getting dressed in the morning and getting stuck in traffic jams. Good-bye, business suits! Good-bye, pantyhose! Hello, slippers and bathrobe, and hello to commuting from bedroom to computer in four minutes. (Hey, had to stop for the morning cup of java, you know.) Gail is going to make sure this will last for the long run. Let the good times roll!

These good times take planning and discipline, however. You are only trading one set of circumstances for another. Telecommuting has provided opportunities for companies and employees alike to take advantage of distant talent. Employees can work at their own paces and set their own schedules as long as deadlines are met and commitments are kept. Employers get happier employees who produce more and are less stressed.

The danger in telecommuting is that if you are looking for promotion opportunities, critical face time evaporates. The adage, "out of sight, out of mind," fits here. So if promotions are important to you, think carefully about how to remain "visible" to the necessary people in your organization. You've worked hard to establish your 4C Image, and you don't want to lose your leverage.

Home-based Business

Let's look at another scenario.

After careful pondering, Evan made a decision that will change his and his family's lives forever. There was no turning back. You see, Evan, vice president of operations for a large packaging firm, was in line for promotion to the top spot in his organization, but over the past year, Evan has been unsettled. Yes, his corporate goal of becoming the company's youngest CEO was in his grasp, but in his heart, he knew that it would be a hollow triumph. He ached to have his own business and spend more time with his wife and young kids.

Evan's true love was gardening and landscape design, having minored in horticulture while in college. His free time, what little he had, was spent working in the garden with the family. Together they planted and nurtured the fruit and vegetables that the family ate year-round. His wife,

Debbie, became an expert at canning and sold her goods at the local farmer's market for the fun of it. Evan loved teaching the children about the earth and what it could produce when cultivated. He reveled in watching the expressions of his children and sharing their excitement as they watched their seeds grow into beautiful plants.

Evan's talent showed in the beautiful landscaping around his home. It was so spectacular that several friends and colleagues commissioned him to landscape their new homes and their businesses. Evan's work received high acclaim from all that saw it, and he was often told that he was in the wrong business.

Back in the office, Evan realized that his feelings toward his work had changed. As a leader, he was well respected in his own company and throughout the business community. He never compromised his reputation of providing superior customer service to his employees and paying customers. For Evan, though, it was not enough. He longed to experience the same excitement that his kids did when they gardened together. Evan decided to become his own best customer by being true to himself. So he left his high-paying job to establish a new enterprise, Evan's Landscape Design, Inc., with corporate headquarters in his basement.

These two very different scenarios share one idea. Both Gail and Evan will be working out of their home offices. The following information from *Success* magazine illustrates that they are not alone:

From Success Magazine

■ Independent workers now comprise one-third of the U.S. labor force. By the year 2000, they are projected to be a majority of the nation's total workforce.
(Source: Independent Workers Association)

■ The total number of home-based workers is 47 million, an increase of 50% since 1989; of these, more than 14.2 million are self-employed.
(Source: FIND/SVP, *Success*, 1996)

■ Today, the SOHO (Small Office/Home Office) market sector is growing at an annual rate of 5% compared to just 3% for the overall American economy.
(Source: Income Opportunities, IDC/LINK Resources, 1996)

■ The *Wall Street Journal* estimates that home-based businesses will spend more than $20 billion on products and services by the year 2000.
(Source: Income Opportunities, IDC/LINK Resources, 1996)

■ Telecommunications companies anticipate that 35% of their growth at the end of this decade will come from home-based businesses.
(Source: Income Opportunities, IDC/LINK Resources, 1996)

■ A self-employed person using a personal computer generates $70,000 in income annually—42% more than the person without a personal computer.
(Source: *Inc. Technology*, February 1995)

■ The top 10 home-based businesses include:
❑ Business consulting and services
❑ Computer services and programming
❑ Financial consulting and services
❑ Marketing and advertising
❑ Medical practices and services
❑ Graphics and visual arts
❑ Public relations
❑ Real estate
❑ Writing
❑ Independent sales
(Source: IDC/LINK, *Success*, 1996)

RESIDENCE/OFFICE LINE

Today's home office requires a telephone line, telephone, fax machine, computer, modem, answering machine or service, and e-mail. These tools provide the necessary resources to effectively deliver your work from and to any location electronically. Working successfully from home, either for yourself or someone else, requires replicating the business tools in the company office in order to maintain the same level of quality and professionalism in your work. Make sure that you read the ideas in Chapter 4 on how to set up your office. Whether the office is located in a home or office building, the principles are the same. The rest of this chapter will provide you with information on how to present a professional telephone image when working from home.

How Many Lines?

How many telephone lines does a home-based business or telecommuting setup require? That certainly depends on your needs. If you don't fax or use the Internet frequently, you may be able to get by with one line at first. Many businesses that approve telecommuting will pick up the tab for extra phone lines, so make sure that you ask what equipment they will provide.

Conflict results when other family members want to use the phone and you are "on-line" on the Internet, faxing, or speaking with a client. If the short five-minute call to your client or your boss evolves into a forty-five-minute diatribe, other family members may not be too understanding, especially the teenaged group.

Some telephone companies offer a service called Ringmate, where you have up to three different telephone numbers coming into one line. Each number has its own distinctive ring, so you know who the call is for. This doesn't answer the problem of angry teens when you're on the phone, but at least you'll know when not to answer the phone if it's their "ring."

Adding a second line offers flexibility and avoids family conflicts. Eventually, you may want to dedicate a line solely for the residence and two others for your home office: one for business and the other for the fax/modem.

Multiple lines offer the advantage of making and accepting calls while faxing and when working "side by side" with clients on the Internet. What if you're working on a major project with your client, whose office is in California, and you are in New York? With the Internet, you can both look at the same image at the same time on your computer screens while discussing the project on the telephone. This scenario would be impossible with a single phone line in your home office. Multiple lines help you appear more professional by allowing you to use modern technology to its fullest. It helps you provide the best product along with the best customer service.

The Home Office Answering Service

Not being able to leave telephone messages sends a clear signal to bosses and clients that they are dealing with someone who is unprofessional, incompetent, and lacking in credibility. Why so harsh? Think about it. With any business, if clients can't connect with you because they hear a continuous busy signal or ringing, they wonder if you really exist. They then go to the next person on the list. That's a loss businesses cannot afford. If you are a telecommuter and your boss can't connect with you because of a busy signal, then it may be good-bye to your new freedom. If you were in your boss's shoes and you couldn't connect with your employee, wouldn't you consider that the employee was off vacationing in Tahiti instead of working? A professional person provides a way for callers to leave messages twenty-four hours a day. It's part of the 4C Image.

You have a choice of four methods that will ensure you present a 4C Image.

Call Answering Service The local telephone company provides this service for a monthly fee. The beauty of it lies in its ability to take messages behind the scenes while you are conversing with a client. There's comfort in knowing that anyone else who calls in can leave messages without interrupting you. You can retrieve your messages or change your greeting from anywhere by calling a central number and entering a password. Unfortunately, there's no blinking light telling you that a message is waiting. You'll need to train yourself to pick up the phone occasionally and check for the stutter that signals you have received messages. Also, you can't screen messages as they are being left because you can't hear the message being delivered. You have to wait until the caller finishes. Then you must dial into the message center to retrieve the new message.

Answering Service Many people are tired of leaving messages on machines, so hearing a live human voice can make you look good. However, it can also make you look bad if the service employees are not trained properly. Before you hire this type of service, check it out carefully. Call several times and evaluate how they answer the phone and take messages. Remember: They are representing you. Whether they present a 4C Image or an unprofessional image reflects on you. Most of these services are professional and efficient, and their people are well trained.

Answering Machine These machines are inexpensive, come in all shapes, and have all sorts of features. You can definitely find a machine that fits your needs and budget. With many systems, you may retrieve your messages and change your greeting remotely. Most have some sort of visual signal, such as a blinking light, that alerts you there are messages. A number counter indicates how many messages you have waiting. These machines are ideal for screening calls. The telephone etiquette section of this chapter will fill you in on dos and don'ts of using this machine.

Beeper/Pager System Beepers, also known as pagers, are wonderful little creatures that attach to your waistband or are carried in a pocket or purse. Beepers help keep parents in touch with kids, expectant fathers in touch with ready-to-deliver moms, companies in touch with employees, and salespeople and entrepreneurs in touch with clients. They are a surefire way to keep communication lines open, if only we remember to take them with us. Refer to Chapter 3 for more information on beepers.

Call waiting and three-way calling are two more useful services for maintaining professionalism in the home-based office.

Busy signals are almost a thing of the past with call waiting. Here's how it works. A distinct tone signals that you have another call. You then place the first call on hold, and answer the second call by pressing the receiver button or the flash button. To go back to your first call, you repeat the process. This wonderful service can be abused and work against you if it is not used wisely. Be sure to read the following etiquette section in this chapter to pick up some dos and don'ts for call waiting.

If your telephone system does not have a conferencing feature, then this service comes in handy for the home office. It lets the user talk simultaneously with two other people in separate locations. You can use it for brainstorming sessions, planning sessions, and anytime you don't want to repeat yourself twice.

HOME OFFICE PHONE ETIQUETTE

Answering Calls

Answering the telephone in your home office should be no different than answering it in the workplace. Remember:

The better you sound when answering the phone, the more positive your caller's first impression will be. Answering with a simple *Hello* doesn't work. It gives a lightweight feeling, and you do not connect with the caller. Whether or not you have a dedicated line, use a greeting such as:

> *Hello, this is Evan, how may I help you?*

You may consider saying your business name first. For example:

> *Evan's Landscape Design, Ivy speaking, how may I help you?*

A more formal greeting would include a connection phrase such as *Good morning* or *Thank you for calling*. The greeting would then be worded as follows:

> *Good morning, Skip and Flip, Inc., this is Gail, how may I help you?*

Don't forget to use your mirror. We talked about it in Chapter 4, remember? Put it up so that you can see yourself clearly. Whether you are a telecommuter or home business, the customer must always hear that smile. If you work with any of the teleconferencing tools that were discussed in Chapter 5, use your mirror not only to check out your smile, but also to check out what you look like. You don't want your boss or client to see you working in your nice fuzzy bathrobe and Barney slippers.

Receiving Calls

Answering machines are great if used well. Unfortunately, some people insist on using cute little greetings recorded by their children, jokes that not everyone understands, weird music, or flip greetings such as "You know what to do." Sorry, but this doesn't cut it in the business world. You wouldn't leave such a greeting on the workplace telephone system, so why do it in your home office? It's a turnoff and unprofessional. People have lost job opportunities because the caller deemed what they considered funny inappropriate. Think clearly about the impression you wish to form in the caller's mind with your greeting. Pay close attention to your tone of voice and the words you use. It may be the first interaction the caller has with you and your business. Those first few seconds tell a whole lot about you, so make the most of it.

Write out your greeting before you record it. Use a natural-sounding voice, and try not to sound as if you're reading a script. Create your own personalized greeting by following the basic examples below. Be creative if you choose, but be careful.

> **Telecommuter:** *Hi, this is Gail. I'm not available at the moment, but your call is important to me. Please leave your name, telephone number, and a detailed message, and I'll return your call as soon as possible.*
>
> **Home Business:** *Thank you for calling Evan's Landscape Design. We are either on another line or away from our desks. Please leave your name, telephone number, and a detailed message, and we'll return your call as soon as possible.*

Screening Calls

If you must screen your calls using an answering machine, be careful. It's easy to abuse call screening, and it can give your customer a negative feeling if you use it frequently, especially with repeat customers. Here's an example of how not to use call screening:

A couple wanted to adopt a child internationally. After much research, they hired an agency that came highly recommended. The agency was a home-based business run out of the director's home. Most of the time the service was good, but the agency had one bad habit that made the couple wonder, even after all their research, if it was legitimate. The agency screened every call. Regardless of when the couple contacted the agency, the answering machine always answered. Midway through the message, the director would pick up the phone. It became annoying. Those times when the calls weren't picked up, the couple wondered if the director was indeed there and listening, but didn't want to answer the call. The agency's telephone behavior evoked two responses:

- I'm glad that I'm important enough for you to pick up the phone! (sarcastic)
- Who are you avoiding? (mistrust)

This latter reaction led to a feeling of distrust that was difficult to shake.

So what's the moral of the story? Answer calls personally whenever possible. Hearing a live human voice versus a recording really makes a difference. If you are working and don't want to be disturbed, let the service or machine take the message. It's always best to let the caller leave a message and return the call later.

Call Waiting: Friend or Foe?

Call waiting can be your salvation. Yes, you won't miss a call, but if used unwisely, you may lose business. When you are speaking with a client, especially if the client has called you and it's his "nickel," it's rude to answer another incoming call. So what do you do? Let the local telephone company's call answering service take the message. By signing up for both call waiting and call answering service, you earn flexibility. You show respect to your caller by not interrupting the conversation, and the other caller has the opportunity to leave a message with the call answering service. This combination creates a win-win situation for everyone. If you choose, you have the option of temporarily turning off call waiting by pressing * 70. If you leave it on, you will be able to count how many calls you received during the conversation.

If you must answer the call waiting tone:

■ Always ask permission first from the person with whom you are speaking.

■ Show respect by saying *May I please put you on hold?* versus *Hold on*. This person may understand your voice tone and know that you are answering an incoming call.

■ Don't make statements such as, "Let me get rid of this call." This is a demeaning and negative comment and signals to the person on hold that the person calling in is a bother. He may be thinking, "Do you say the same thing about me when you're on a call with someone else?"

When answering the second call:

■ Deliver your greeting.

■ Ask the second caller for her name and phone number.

■ Ask for the best times to either return the call or for her to call you back.

■ Return to the first caller and thank him for holding.

If you do not have call waiting or the call answering service and you have another line for your fax/modem, you are in luck.

■ Attach an answering machine to the main line.

■ Use the fax line to make your outgoing calls, and let the machine answer incoming calls on the other line. If you can, turn down the ring volume on the answering machine's line so the ring doesn't distract you from your call. Remember that you won't be able to send or receive faxes or get on-line during that time.

KIDS, PHONES, AND THE HOME OFFICE

As engineering manager of a large company, Jim realized that his people were having problems connecting with a new client's personnel. Communications were getting crossed and tempers were flaring, which put the contract in jeopardy. Jim's boss handed him a brochure from a consulting company that might be able to help them. The brochure was professionally done and described just the services that Jim was looking for, so he decided to call. Imagine his surprise when he was greeted with "mama bye-bye, I wuv you too!" and a loud click.

Thinking the first call was a fluke, Jim called again. This time the line was busy. The baby probably left the phone off the hook. Not very impressive. He put the brochure away intending to try later in the day.

Two days later, Jim finally got around to making the call again. This time he heard a greeting that said, "Sorry, we're busy. Please call back." The lack of congruency between the professionalism of the brochure and the telephone responses Jim received lost the consultants a potentially lucrative deal. The worst part was that the consulting company didn't even know that the engineering firm had called!

The consulting company had not done its homework and had not prepared itself properly to handle the telephone portion of its business. As stated earlier, 50 percent of business is done over the telephone. Let's focus on how to avoid these mistakes.

If you are fortunate enough to have a secluded room for your home office, count your lucky stars. Many offices, set up on the kitchen or dining room table, have no doors to separate them from the rest of the household. Ideally, you should set up your office in a room with a door and separate telephone line. However, that's not always possible. This presents challenges that can drive the entrepreneur or the telecommuter batty. It's most difficult to present a 4C Image to callers when:

■ There are babies crying in the background.

■ Your seven-year-old wants to show you her latest drawing…now!

■ Your teenager is asking for the car keys while you are speaking with the representative from your largest account.

■ You answer the phone and it's a new prospect. In horror, you realize that the clock on your computer reads 4 p.m. and, at any moment, the kids will come home from school screaming through the back door. Before you are able to say, "May I return your call," they arrive, and you frantically, silently, and ineffectively wave your arms to get them to be quiet.

Home Office Tips for Presenting a 4C Image

A few home office telephone tips to consider:

■ **Plan a specific time to make your calls**. If you have young children, wait until they are napping or at nursery school. If possible, hire a baby-sitter to take the kids out or watch them in another part of the house. During that time, you can completely focus on calls without distractions. Consider starting a baby-sitting co-op with other home-based businesses in your area.

- **Place your telephone where little hands can't get to it**. A telephone can be inviting to little ones who think it's just another toy. They don't realize it's a valuable toy for "big kids." Also, telephones with long cords are safety hazards, so it's best to keep them high and out of the way.

- **Use an alarm**. If possible, avoid taking or answering calls at the precise time the children get home from school. Program your computer alarm, or an alarm clock, to alert you when it's five minutes before the kids' arrival time.

- **Use a portable telephone**. With a portable phone, you can move to a quiet part of the house to speak with your colleagues and clients, but beware of cell phone abuse! When working from home, the temptation to fix the plumbing, vacuum the floor, or make the beds can really get the best of us. Portable phones have given us so much flexibility that we are tempted to do our housekeeping while on the phone with a client. Don't give in to the temptation. You don't want your client listening to a toilet flushing during your conversation.

- **Train your children (and spouse) how to answer the phone**. What a gift to give your children for the future! Think of the impressive image that they will present to their employers when they already know how to answer the phone and take messages properly.

You may ask, "Train the spouse?" Well, yes, especially if the spouse has not been in a situation where he or she must answer the phone professionally. They represent you, and how they answer the phone creates a positive or negative image for your business. Just saying *hello* lacks the professionalism that customers are expecting.

If your kids aren't old enough to take messages, teach them to answer the phone only when you are in the house. In this way, the child can get you instead of attempting to take a message. A colleague's daughter wanted to answer the phone when she was three years old. She and her parents made a deal: She had to do it Mom's way or not at all. To this day, she answers the phone with:

Hello, this is Katie, how may I help you?

For safety's sake, children learn in school not to say their names over the telephone. If you feel uncomfortable having your children use their names when answering the phone, have them use a greeting such as:

Thank you for calling Cornball Enterprises, may I help you?

This greeting helps the caller to connect, and it's easy enough that your child can learn it quickly. Once the child hears what the caller wants, she says:

One moment please, or *May I put you on hold?*

Then she goes to get her mother.

Katie had to be taught, though, not to put the phone down and scream at the top of her lungs, "MOM, IT'S FOR YOU!" If your phone has a hold button, show your child where it is and how to use it. Make sure that the child clearly understands that she must get you immediately. More than once, clients have been left on hold way too long because the child got distracted by a TV show or went outside to pick daisies in the garden.

Katie, now ten, continues to impress callers with her telephone skills. When her mother is asked how her daughter does it, Mom's simple response is: "I taught her."

CHAPTER SEVEN

Contagious Enthusiasm: Catch It and Pass It On!

You are now aware of how easily your telephone image can influence how others respond to you. You've learned skills to help you present yourself with a 4C Image to your coworkers, staff, and customers. One area remains to be addressed: your attitude. Attitude is an infectious word, the power of which should never be underestimated. Attitude comes in two flavors: negative and positive. Both affect the heart, mind, and soul of an organization and its people.

Like a polluted waterfall, a negative attitude, accompanied by negative actions and words, can wash over everyone and create an unpleasant environment with little trust, honor, and respect. As with water, negativism will fill every nook and cranny, making itself heard and felt over a telephone, in person, and in writing.

Contagious Enthusiasm

C ommunicate with power and integrity to everyone who crosses your path. We can all learn from one another if we choose to listen carefully.

O utstanding achievements are made when you put your heart and soul into everything you do.

N egotiate to create win-win situations.

T each yourself to look carefully at what's around you, to listen well, to feel others' words and emotions, and to learn from the actions of others. Be fully present in the moment.

A ctions reflect your thoughts and feelings. Take responsibility for making them positive ones.

G enuine concern for others, regardless of your position, is a sign of a true leader.

I nnovate to stay ahead of the competition.

O rganize yourself and your life so that your energy flows freely.

U nify your thoughts, words, and actions to present a congruent (harmonious) image.

S atisfaction comes with hard work and a positive attitude.

E nergize by taking care of yourself. Take time to rest, exercise, eat right, and treat your body with respect.

N otice those around you. Give words of encouragement to everyone, especially those having a bad day.

T rust your instincts to help you make the right decisions.

H onor the thoughts and beliefs of those around you. We are each entitled to our own opinions.

U nderstand yourself first, then learn to understand others.

S hare your knowledge. We each have different experiences from which others can learn.

I nspire through your actions and words.

A ttitude is a choice. Regardless of your circumstances, you decide whether to have a positive or negative attitude.

S mile at everyone who crosses your path. It's your most powerful tool.

M e. The person you choose to be. It starts and ends with you. The choice is yours.

A positive attitude, on the other hand, creates a pristine waterfall of positive actions and words. Such energy generates an inviting environment in which employees and customers alike are valued and welcomed. My colleagues at R.C. Taylor and Associates call this *Positude*®.

What makes attitude, positive or negative, so contagious? Think of the word contagious and you immediately think of disease. After all, what's more contagious than the common cold? The negative energy of the word sends you running in the opposite direction. In contrast, enthusiasm creates an image of positive energy and passion, and that draws you in. Who doesn't smile at the thought of little children enthusiastically diving into bowls of their favorite ice cream? Pair the word "contagious" with the word "enthusiasm" and a transformation occurs. A positive and high-energy contrast, contagious enthusiasm brings to life an image of smiling happy people who are enjoying what they're doing and influencing others along the way. Whether in person or over the telephone, we all have the power to create contagious enthusiasm by implementing guidelines on the facing page.

Remember . . .

Your Telephone Image Says So Much About You!

I dentify your customer's needs.
M ake sure you are smiling.
A ppreciate your customer's loyalty.
G reet your customer with warmth.
E xceed your customer's expectations.

With Positude!
Terry

Resources

Business By Phone

13254 Stevens Street
Omaha, NE 68137
Voice: (800) 326-7721
E-mail: Art@businessbyphone.com
http://www.businessbyphone.com
Art Sobczak

Tele-Smart Communications

1491 17th Avenue
San Francisco, CA 94122
Voice: (415) 759-6537
Fax: (415) 759-9873
E-mail: josiane@telsmart.com
http://www.tele-smart.com
Josiane Feigon

The Marketing Coach

514 Daniels Street, #299
Raleigh, NC 27605
Voice: (919) 834-8999
Fax: (919) 836-1211
Email: Leslie@themarketingcoach.com
http://www.themarketingcoach.com
Leslie Speidel, President

Peer Resources

Development and Mentoring for
    Schools and Business
1052 Davie Street
Victoria, British Columbia V8S 4E3
Voice: (250) 595-3503
Fax: (250) 595-3504
E-mail: rcarr@islandnet.com
http://www.islandnet.com/~rcarr/
    peer.html
Rey A. Carr, Ph.D.

R.C. Taylor and Associates

Training and Development
125 Commons Court
Chadds Ford, PA 19317
Voice: (610) 558-9200
Fax: (610) 558-4708
E-mail: RCTYLR@aol.com
http://www.tregistry.com/ttr/
    rctaylor.htm
Roseanne and Jeff Taylor

TTI Performance Systems, Ltd.

16020 N. 77th Street
Scottsdale, AZ 85260
Voice: (800) 869-6908
Fax: (800) 788-3472
E-mail: tti@ttidisc.com
http://www.ttidisc.com
Rick Bowers

8x8, Inc.

2445 Mission College Boulevard
Santa Clara, CA 95054
Voice: (408) 727-1885
Fax: (408) 980-0432
http://www.8x8.com

Hello Direct

5893 Rue Ferrari
San Jose, CA 95138-1857
(800) 444-3556
Fax: (800) 456-2566
E-mail: xpressit@hihello.com
http://www.hello-direct.com
Telephone products and accessories